Also by Bro. Vance Moore
From Indigo Sea Press

Critical Presence: It's a God Thang

indigoseapress.com

Critical Presence: Love God, Love Y'all, That's All

By

Bro. Vance Moore

Clear Light Books
Published by Indigo Sea Press
Winston-Salem

Clear Light Books
Indigo Sea Press
PO Box 26701
Winston-Salem, NC 27114

Copyright 2020 by Bro. Vance Moore
All rights reserved, including the right of reproduction in whole or part in any format.

First Clear Light Books edition published
March, 2020
Clear Light Books, Moon Sailor and all production design are trademarks of Indigo Sea Press, used under license.

For information regarding bulk purchases of this book, digital purchase and special discounts, please contact the publisher at indigoseapress@gmail.com

Cover Concept by Bro. Vance Moore
Cover design by Pan Morelli
Manufactured in the United States of America

ISBN 978-1-63066-484-8

Dedication.

Over the years, God has blessed me with some of the most incredible folks; to those whom I know as Brothers and Sisters in Christ, I say thank-you for being my Brother or Sister by walking the path with me!

Over the years, God has blessed me with Divine Appointments. They belong to Him and Him alone. He blessed me with the privilege of serving them in some way, always in His name. Thank You Father

To my Gwen, I dedicate this as well. Together our Lord is blessing us in our golden years. Love God, Love Y'all, That's All. Hang on! God Ain't done with us yet!

Critical Presence: Love God, Love Y'all, That's All

Introduction

We thought our mission work story was finished, only to discover a new chapter was just beginning. My wife Gwen and I decided we would stop on a Sunday morning and worship with old friends in Hattiesburg, Mississippi. We had just finished a fifteen-month pastorate at Yellow Pine Christian Church (Disciples of Christ) in Sibley, Louisiana. During that period the membership of the congregation had grown from fifteen to eighty-four. While fulfilling, the work had been arduous, and we decided the time had come to retire from the ministry.

It wasn't the first time I had made that decision. After all, since retiring as a businessman and contractor, I had served a number of very different ministries. Along with my late wife Jeannie, I had been a bi-vocational pastor and Christian educator in Arkansas.

Early in 2006 I accepted a call to the Westside Christian Church in Algiers, Louisiana, that involved rebuilding both the church building and the congregation after Hurricane Katrina. We had founded the Westside Christian Mission and brought in thousands of volunteers from across the nation to help rebuild the New Orleans area.

After our work concluded at Westside, I was asked to become a Regional Pastor for the Great River Region, which includes the states of Arkansas, Louisiana and Mississippi. I semi-retired from that position in 2012 and assumed the pastorate of Yellow Pine Christian Church in northwest Louisiana.

At last, at the end of February, 2014, I retired once more—this time, I thought, for good. The following week we planned a trip from Minden, Louisiana, where we lived to visit family in New Orleans. We were going to travel back through

Mississippi on our way and decided to stop in Hattiesburg for Sunday worship. There was a congregation there, Central Christian Church, with which I was well-acquainted from my time as a Regional Pastor. I knew the church's pastor, Norman Sanders, who had been serving Central for ten years. I also had a long-time acquaintance in the congregation, the church's organist Sharon Royalty. She and I and gone to high school together in 1964.

I gave Sharon a courtesy phone call to share with her that Gwen and I would be attending worship. During our conversation, Sharon told me that, ironically, Norm had resigned after the third Sunday of February. She asked me if I would consider bringing the message when we came. This phone call was taking place on Saturday. She was asking me to preach the next day. I agreed and on that first Sunday of March, I preached at Central Christian Church. There were twelve or thirteen people in attendance that Sunday. One of the members requested that we offer a prayer for healing, which we were delighted to share.

After we returned to Minden, Sharon called. She said one of the elders wanted to talk to me and asked if she could share our phone number with Marilyn Williams, who promptly called. Her question to me was straightforward, "Can you help us?" We had a lengthy conversation. She explained that, from the time they knew Norman was leaving, they had not been able to secure anyone to preach. They were really in need of help. She asked me if I could assist.

I did not give her a direct answer. I told her only that I would come the following week and bring the message again. At that time Gwen and I had agreed we had no intention or desire to enter into another pastorate for the foreseeable future. Still, here were Christians asking for help. I told Marilyn I would come for one month and fill the pulpit. My intent was strictly to do pulpit supply for one month. During that time, Gwen and I continued to live in Minden. We made the trip—

Critical Presence: Love God, Love Y'all, That's All

a five-hour one-way drive—in mid to late week. I thought it was just going to be a really long, month of travel. Soon I realized, however, that this pulpit supply would become the next "God Thang" in my life.

As I have said and written repeatedly, I don't believe God closes churches. People, however, do close churches, and pretty much always for the same reason: because their efforts at revitalization fail. During my work with the many churches who came to Westside Mission Center to help rebuild New Orleans, and also in my Regional Pastor efforts with the small churches in the Great River Region, I had grown troubled at the efforts of our denomination in trying—but not succeeding—to revitalize the small churches. It is not my intention to criticize the denomination. Based on my observations, however, there was no denying that our denominational attempts at revitalization did not bode well for the small churches. Indeed, over the years, many of those congregations closed. If there was ever a church ripe to be closed, surely it was Central Christian Church of Hattiesburg.

Central Christian wasn't the first congregation in this condition to which I had ministered. Westside Christian Church had been in decline before Hurricane Katrina destroyed the facility and dispersed the membership. Yellow Pine had dwindled to less than twenty members before Gwen and I arrived. I think it's essential to note, though, that while many declining churches face similar issues, no two congregations are alike. Recognizing this, I knew my first task was to resist prejudging the church and the issues it was facing.

I had this in mind the next week when Gwen and I returned to lead worship at Central Christian Church. We were warmly received and it was evident to me but God was calling us there. I did not know what He was saying. I knew from many "God Thang" happenings in the past that my sole priority was to put one foot in front of the other and listen—listen to the members of the church and to whatever the Holy Spirit might say.

Frankly, most of what we heard and learned at first was discouraging. Like Westside, Central Christian in Hattiesburg was considered a "dying church." In its heyday, the congregation had an active membership of about 150. When Gwen and I arrived, the membership had dwindled to fifteen. And those few members were mostly older adults. The majority of the members were over seventy, with several in their eighties and with some approaching their nineties. There were no young people apart from one twenty-year-old young man and his brother, thirty-six, along with a new member in her forties.

Central Christian, Hattiesburg, Mississippi

Critical Presence: Love God, Love Y'all, That's All

As if it weren't discouraging enough that we had very few members, our numbers immediately began to shrink. Within a short period of time we lost several members who moved out of the area. One elderly woman remarried and moved to her membership to her new husband's church. Even my friend Sharon Royalty retired and moved to Florida. We had started with fifteen and suddenly found ourselves only with eleven. Thankfully, no member yet passed on to the Eternal Church. Then there was the financial issue. It had been many, many months since Central Christian had enough income to meet its budgetary requirements. In order to pay its monthly expenses, the church was forced to draw upon its limited reserves. The Sunday service was now being held in the fellowship hall, not the sanctuary, in order to keep utility cost down.

With all these considerations weighing upon us, I found myself reflecting on my previous ministerial experiences, all of which seemed to begin in the midst of overwhelming hardship. My time as director of Westside Mission Center was concluded in 2010. My time as a regional Pastor for the Great River Region was concluded in 2012. I was the pastor of Yellow Pine Christian Church in Sibley, Louisiana, until the third week of February, 2014. The successful revitalization experienced by the Yellow Pine Christian Church during our fifteen months there renewed my zeal for both small church ministry and for congregational revitalization ministry. Of course, revitalizing another declining small church was not on our minds when we planned our Sunday stop in Hattiesburg. On the final week of February, 2014, I just wanted to go to church and worship. It was so much to think about and to pray about.

In the end, however, we could not deny that this was clearly another one of those God Thangs. So, at the end of the first week in March I told them I would come and that I would serve in a temporary capacity for a period of one month in order to give them some time to plan their next moves.

Transitions like this are seldom as simple as they might seem. At that time the former pastor was still residing in the parsonage. Gwen and I spent the next three weeks staying with Marilyn Williams at her home during the three days each week we were in town.

Immediately we began getting to know the congregation and to understand its particular processes. Our meetings with Marilyn and with other members of the church revealed some interesting dynamics. Over a period of time they had endured multiple attempts to move the congregation to a new location and or even to close the church. The members were adamant that they had no intention of leaving their present location, where they had worshipped for 107 years. Moreover, they certainly had no interest in closing the church. In the face of this was the undeniable downside of their limited financial reserves, and the fact that they were dipping into those reserves on a monthly basis just to pay their regular bills.

As that one month to which we had committed progressed, I began to understand God was calling me to this church in order to revitalize and rebuild Central Christian Church. Because I had served this congregation in the past as their Regional Pastor, I chose to involve Barbara Jones, the Great River Regional Minister in the meeting that I requested with the church at the end of March, 2014.

One of the few stipulations that I placed upon my accepting the call to become the pastor of this church was that we would not under any circumstances use any more of their reserves to pay the congregation's regular expenses. I agreed to become the fulltime Central Christian Church Pastor and to be compensated in the amount of $16,000 per year. In the five-and-a-half years I have been the pastor of Central, we have not once dipped into the reserve fund.

As I mentioned before, when we began our ministry, there were fifteen members. That number quickly dropped to eleven. Yet we survived. Within a few weeks, we had a couple new members join and a couple old members return. Soon we were back to sixteen. Today, five-and-a-half years later, we are beginning to grow in earnest.

Central Christian Sanctuary

Back in those first days, however, we quickly discovered one of the most remarkable traits about the church's membership: these folks are incredibly dependable. They are there every week. Not only does a dependable congregation inspire its pastor, but it makes engaging the membership and starting mission work so much simpler and more effective.

I liken revitalizing a church to turning a 600-foot luxury liner around in the Mississippi River. It can't be done. You have to back it out into the Gulf of Mexico, turn it around and reenter the river. Today we've turned our ship around and we're headed upstream. Praise God!

Today we count forty active members. All our members are active, even though some of them are homebound. Those who are unable to come to worship still participate in the life of the church through their contributions and by being connected to their church in a variety of ways. Twenty-five of those forty are in church almost every Sunday. The numbers may be small but the percentage of members who attend worship is phenomenal.

As mentioned before, while there are great similarities among small, declining congregations, no two churches are alike—even those whose membership has dwindled. Someone might ask, accordingly, what is unique about Central Christian Church? I've reflected about this a great deal in the months since I became the congregation's pastor. I think I can answer that question by saying, in addition to their amazing commitment and dependability, these Christians had every reason to give up and shut down this church. Closing God's church, however, was never an option for these folks.

Before God sent Gwen and me there, they had no idea how they could survive. They had no idea where they could find a pastor. Then God sent us. One of my members, Bobby West, who is in his early 80s now, tells people there is one thing of which he is sure: God sent Vance Moore to be the pastor of Central Christian Church. When I hear him say that, I am humbled.

Remembering this takes me back to that time when Jeannie went home to Jesus, I asked God to take me too—unless, and only if, he wanted me to stay here to let me serve

Critical Presence: Love God, Love Y'all, That's All

him in a way that counted. I felt God's answer to that prayer during my time as the director of the mission center. I felt when I was serving in the position of Great River Regional Pastor. I felt it in my time at Sibley. Now I feel it deeply at Central Christian Church.

When I consider the future of the church today, one of the conundrums I have struggled with throughout my ministry is this: why do we as the church allows small congregations to die. I realize that this is something that the church itself has struggled with. I have now come to believe that Critical Presence can be lived out by going back to The Basics. By that I mean listening to Christ and following his lead in our daily walk.

One of the practical ways to achieve this is Bible study. If we learn, discern, and internalize how He is leading us in our spiritual walk then things of worship, mission, evangelism as well as all things spiritual will naturally follow. With that in mind I see the next move in my call to be developing a Bible study teaching The Basics.

As with any other discipline, learning The Basics is paramount. As always, Jesus touches my heart with simplicity. HE touched me with HIS word, "Love the Lord your God with all your heart and with all your soul and with all your mind. This is the first and greatest commandment. And the second is like it: Love your neighbor as yourself. All the law and the Prophets hand on these two commandments." I coined a phrase, "Love God, Love Y'all, That's All." It says it all for me.

It is my belief that God's call is the intersection of need and willingness. We live in a changed broken world today. You have only to turn the 6 o'clock news and be instantly pulled into an environment of hate, dissention, polarization and all things the opposite of Love God, Love Y'all, That's All. I have learned that God will provide the tools that you need to answer any call He places upon your heart. When you, as Christ's servant, arrive at the intersection of need and willingness, your job is to provide openness and acceptance. The need is easy to see—IF WE ARE TO BE THE PEOPLE JESUS IS CALLING US TO BE, WE MUST LEARN TO LOVE GOD, AND LOVE EACH OTHER ABOVE ALL.

My first thirty days at Central Christian Church was my first God Thang experience with this particular congregation. God revealed his will to me in the openness of the members, and in their willingness to serve.

There are many differences between Westside Mission Center and small church ministry. There are also similarities. It could be said that volunteers came to the Westside Mission Center needing to experience God. It was at Westside and the aftermath of the ravages of Hurricane Katrina that I lived the experiences of Love God, Love Y'all, That's All. It was when we, yes we (ALL OF US), stood in the midst of total loss of everything, that we began to see; color no longer mattered, social status was blown away literally in the ruins of possessions; wealth taken away in the span of a few hours, we experienced being reduced to our basic humanness, it was then, when we began to sense the beauty of our God, standing tall, standing strong, standing in LOVE. It somewhat reminds me of the final verse of 1 Corinthians 13, "and now these three remain: faith, hope, and love. But the greatest of these is love."

Now, years later, back in the small church community, I realized it could also be said that the members of a small church come to church on Sunday needing to experience God. And both of these are true. My experience with ministry at Westside Mission Center and in the small church is that they are both the essence of Critical Presence. Yes, Critical Presence is meeting people at their point of deepest need and sharing "Love God, Love Y'all, That's All. Until we understand this message from Jesus, we will fail to fully understand God's message and call to his people.

People come to experience God no matter the place. Each of them brings their unique needs. Those unique needs are

Critical Presence: Love God, Love Y'all, That's All

critical to them uniquely and individually. Regardless of the severity of those needs, they are critical to that person. I'm reminded of the scripture in which Christ says he came not to be served but to serve. There is a large life lesson here. This is what *Love God, Love Y'all, That's All* is all about: Basics—Brothers and Sisters in Christ Serving. That was true in the aftermath of hurricane recovery work in a busy place like Westside Mission Center, and it's equally true in every church, large or small, and in any interaction between Christians and other people—Christian and non-Christian alike, all human beings.

When I arrived at Central Christian Church there was a survival mindset and that was good. However, that "survive" mindset had to morph into a "thrive" mindset. There is a lot of difference in the approach for churches in different stages of their life cycle. Ours, according to the experts, was in the decline cycle. I didn't see it that way then, and I don't see it that way now. I do think that some of our members thought that. I sometimes wonder if they thought that survival meant "keep the church going until I depart for heaven." I knew that had to change. We had to develop the mindset of the church in the future. It's not just the church today.

Years ago I learned a concept from Zig Ziglar. Zig said, you can't get anybody to change their mind about anything, but you can get them to make a new decision based on new information. Our members needed some new information.

One thing I was taught early on in my ministry was that one should be careful to not make new changes in the first months of your ministry. Still, I needed to do something to make a statement. When we arrived at Central the communion table sat way back on the chancel. It seemed to be so far removed from the congregation. The pulpit was raised and seemed to me to be elevated above the members. I moved the communion table down on the floor the sanctuary, close to the members. I came out of the pulpit and now bring the message from in front of the communion table. I ceased to do the service in a robe, which was way too liturgically formal for this small congregation. Everything that I was doing was an attempt to become personal and relational to the church. I needed to help them to sense the Love of Christ in every way God had given me the ability to do and it has worked.

To be sure, there have been many challenges as we've worked to revitalize the church. As with most churches that are dying—who are in the "downside of the bell curve of the life cycle of a church"—there was real lethargy in the day-to-day life of the church. We as a church have spent the last five and-a-half years changing that culture.

When I began this ministry five-and-a-half years ago I knew I had an uphill battle. It was different, very different, from Westside Mission Center. There was a heartfelt desire to continue Central Christian Church. The members had beautiful memories of times past, but as with most older, established churches there was complacency, comfort in the normal routine.

Yet here at Central Christian Church there was that willingness to do what needed to be done in order to truly be God's Church. There was little if any outreach since the congregation couldn't even meet its budget. It's exciting to look today and see us as a supporter of Christian Services, a local Mission Center that helps the poor; to see our Blessing Bag Ministry that provides temporary food bags to homeless; to see our Dog Therapy ladies and their dogs going to *three* nursing homes in the Hattiesburg area and taking God's love to the elderly (Saint Francis is smiling); to see us donating on a regular basis to Jacob's Well, a mission that helps women with substance abuse issues; to see us support Edwards Street Mission, a mission that helps the poor. None of these things were been being done—and now they are being enthusiastically embraced by the members.

Critical Presence: Love God, Love Y'all, That's All

Dog Therapy Group Members

Clearly we've engaged a number of new programs and ministries in our pursuit to revitalize and grow the church. Some worked extremely well while some have not. Without a doubt, however, the number one thing that has made a difference in renewing the congregation has been our Bible study class on Tuesdays. We come together at 10 a.m. for a 30-minute prayer service. Then, from 10:30 to 11:30 we study God's Word. Rather than use the time for the normal Bible study—which covers a large amount of material in a relatively short period of time—we open our Bibles, take scripture and study, share, and pray God's message to each of us. We keep our study method simple.

The Prayer Partner team has breathed new spiritual zest into the group.

We formed a Prayer Partner Team with about ten members five years ago. Today our Prayer Partner meeting average attendance is eighteen committed members. Committed means praying for the names of people on our chronic prayer partner list daily, then discussing and praying together on Tuesdays for these folks. In addition, we bring those names forward on Sunday and lift up those needs at that time also. We utilize our prayer chain via email to lift up needs that come up between meeting times.

Bible study—already Bible study has been a God Thang experience. Most of our members are long-time Christians, which in itself is a blessing and good. Our Bible study is designed to afford each participant the opportunity to develop their discernment and their relationship with Jesus Christ. We don't hurry through a study. When questions arise, we research, discuss, and discern until we are comfortable that we have achieved a greater understanding for all of us. My style of leadership is that of a facilitator. Each participant is encouraged to actively participate in the discussion.

Our knowledge and our coming closer together as a fellowship unit, has enhanced our worship experience for Sunday's. Worship. I use the lectionary as a guideline of scripture. The liturgy places in emphasis of an equal proportion to both the message and the communion table. Within the message there is always intention to be biblically based, telling the story based in its time and then bringing it into today and its meaning for us now.

One of the biggest lessons for me has been recognizing the hunger on the part of long-time church members to go a little deeper into Bible study without becoming "Scholar Nerds"—those who have become inundated with biblical minutia and random information that is more confusing than clarifying for them. There is a balance between real knowledge and understanding and TMI—too much information—for the average person. I am not trying to take away from knowledge in depth. Rather I am saying that Bible study must be journey as well as a destination. Biblical

Critical Presence: Love God, Love Y'all, That's All

discernment is not about impressing congregants with the knowledge of one person, teacher or even facilitator; rather a shared journey in which each member of the group searches for God's truth and how it relates to them. Yes, there is one truth that carries many applications. The beauty of God's word!

The journey of learning the Word of God needs to encompass four elemental questions: First, where did I come from? Second, why am I here? Third, what are my morals and values? Fourth, what is my destiny? My journey to understanding The Basics revealed to me that very few Christians, even those "well-seasoned" in church life, have the answers to those questions and the ability to engage those answer in a practical way. That's what The Basics is all about for me.

Understanding the elements of those four truths will provide a basis for further, more in-depth study of our relationship with Jesus Christ. It is one thing to know something. It is of much more importance to understand why one knows: ergo, The Basics. Often I find myself sitting in a room, teaching a lesson from the Bible and watching the faces of those around me. I can see they are hungry for a deeper relationship with Christ. Teaching the basics is primary, the first step, in that quest.

I hope you enjoy reading *Love God, Love Y'all, That's All*. It will work, if you do! Our God is an awesome God. Living out His command to love Him, love your neighbor and remembering that all the law and all the prophets will forever change and bless your life.

Bro. Vance Moore

Chapter One
Critical Presence

For those hearing it for the first time, the term "Critical Presence" may sound ominous, obscure and baffling. It definitely requires a definition in that it isn't an idea most people are familiar with. Critical Presence has to do with determining a person's point of deepest need; that is, when someone is suffering or lacking, the most important question to ask is, "More than anything else, what does this person need." Proceeding from this idea, there is no attempt to determine whether the person in need is a Christian or a non-Christian, only to determine the individuals of deepest need. Once that need is established, then the next step in Critical Presence is serving that deepest need.

One of the best examples of Critical Presence I've observed was in the ministry shared by thousands of volunteers at Westside Mission in New Orleans Louisiana for the five years following Hurricane Katrina. We did not base any of our volunteer recovery work or assistance to the survivors of Hurricane Katrina upon their religious or spiritual background. We saw people in need, determined their deepest need and we did our best to respond directly to that need.

Another way to gain a clear understanding of Critical Presence is to contrast it to "Colonial Mission" work. Colonial Mission differs from Critical Presence in that the underlying motivation is evangelism. The agape love of Christ is still expressed to people at the point of their deepest need. However with Colonial Mission the underlying priority, heart of the effort, is to establish a Christian Church that will do the evangelistic work of the church.

I saw a good example of this during the time I spent in the Dominican Republic for the Great River Region. We were

Critical Presence: Love God, Love Y'all, That's All

attempting to establish a hands-on working relationship with the *Iglesia de Cristo* church in the Dominican Republic. Our goal was always first and foremost to establish new churches, which obviously required that we do evangelism. We looked at various programs that would speak to the needs of the local community, but the underlying question was always how it impacted the growth of the *Iglesia* Church.

Each of these imperatives, Critical Presence and Colonial Mission, are worthy and honorable objectives for Christians who are reaching out in the name of Jesus Christ to help to heal a broken world. I fully believe in both of these missions. For me and my personal ministerial calling, however, I see an important distinction between serving with Critical Presence as my priority as opposed to serving with Colonial Mission as my intent.

I observed this very significant difference while serving in New Orleans after Hurricane Katrina. I witnessed firsthand how people—both saved and unsaved—can become lost in frustration, fear and need. I saw it, up close and personal, in their eyes, and in their voices. I recognized the depth of the need they were experiencing. Many of these were people of great faith. Many were yearning for more meaningful faith. I saw that even those ones who didn't have a close personal relationship with the Lord were often reaching out for more. I recognized that those who had close personal relationships with their Lord were often finding those relationships challenged. They needed to "see some Jesus" at work around them.

I remember some of the teenager volunteers at the mission center telling me one night, "Brother Vance, we don't want to hear about Jesus. We want to do Jesus." Now that's what I'm talking about: doing Jesus. Almost every one of them was willing to hear about Jesus, but they desperately needed to experience Jesus—up close and personal. That's the kind of deepest need I'm talking about.

Bro. Vance Moore

I have been blessed by serving in Christian ministry for many years. Throughout my ministry, I've had lots of wonderful church members. Many of them wanted to and did participate in mission work, as I did. Still, it was only in the absolute devastation in the streets of New Orleans following Hurricane Katrina that I learned what it meant—the power and importance of this thing we call Critical Presence.

Allow me to share a couple examples of Critical Presence, how it is different and the impact it makes in the lives of those who receive it and those who share it.

Once I had the experience of developing a ministry based on Critical Presence, I knew I wanted this to be the basis of my pastoral work. For instance, in 2012 after I retired as a Regional Pastor for the Great River Region, I felt the call to pastor Yellow Pine Christian Church, the small congregation in Northwestern Louisiana. There in Yellow Pine we lived about thirty-five miles from Shreveport, Louisiana, which meant it was thirty-five miles one way to make hospital visits.

Ironically, once we arrived I began to receive a multitude of phone calls asking for pastoral care. It wasn't long before I realized my being there was a God Thang. People had been waiting for me in a spiritual sense. To be sure, I'd seen so much need in New Orleans. I'd seen so many times God placed people in deep, deep need in my path and into the paths of our volunteers. The concerns were different in Yellow Pine, but the needs were just as deep.

During the fifteen months we served at Yellow Pine, I received many calls from people who were hurting. They had loved ones in the hospital, many of whom were at death's door. The interactions with those in need pretty much always started in the same way: "Pastor I got your name from so-and-so." "You don't know me, but so and so told me you would come to the hospital." "My wife—or my husband or my loved one—is really sick. I don't think they're going to make it." "We don't have anybody to turn to. Would you come?"

Critical Presence: Love God, Love Y'all, That's All

So I went. I sat by the bedside. I prayed with them. I cried with them. In many cases I held the hand of their loved ones as they made that journey, hopefully to the arms of Jesus. They tell me I performed more than twenty funerals during that time. Perhaps. I know I couldn't keep count. But I can tell you what a blessing it was to serve other human beings at their point of deepest need. And I can tell you that some of those folks to whom I ministered ended up in church. Some didn't. There is one thing about which there is no doubt: this was Critical Presence. It's the same ministry those folks in New Orleans experienced. Some believed; some did not. Yet they all had a deep, deep need and at that point they were willing to be filled with love of Jesus Christ. That's the very essence of Critical Presence.

This dynamic has also been at work in Central Christian Church in Hattiesburg, Mississippi. When we arrived there were about fourteen members. Today we're twenty-five strong.

It's a typical church in that so many of downtown churches are on the downside of that bell curve we call the "life of a church." I always thought that was a funny concept. Over the years I learned that churches live, grow, decline and then die. At least, that's according to the experts. I don't claim to understand the experts' methods of determining this, but I do have a deep, abiding belief that God never intended close one church, not one. When the breath of God is breathed into a congregation—just as I have seen it happen repeated in churches where Critical Presence is practiced—it's amazing the new life that erupts in seemingly dying congregations.

Today at Central Christian Church we have a blessing bag ministry. It is a real expression of Critical Presence out in the street where the rubber meets the road: real people who have real needs and Christians reaching out to meet those needs. Here we provide a "therapy dog ministry" to four nursing homes. Talk about Critical Presence! We started with two

Bro. Vance Moore

dogs and three people administering the program. Today we have as many as seven dogs and just as many people going into the nursing homes. Together they are taking love to people who feel they have been thrown away. The faces of the nursing home residents tell the story. We also help to support several other organizations in Hattiesburg—organizations that help people in need by giving a hand up, not a handout.

I say this not to brag but to say, "thank you, Jesus, for beginning to teach us the true meaning of love." And the true meaning of love is expressed through Critical Presence. Our ministry of Critical Presence is not only having an impact on our community, but upon Central Christian itself. If you think about the growth in membership—especially considering the way we lost members at the beginning, we've had numerical growth of about 100% in the time we've been here.

Today, we have forty-five members; we average twenty-five in worship, eighteen people on average in Sunday school and eighteen to twenty people in Bible study, as well and a Prayer Partner group of sixteen to eighteen that meets each Tuesday. We're small, but we're committed. Our Bible study is focused in learning about our true relationship with Jesus. The more we learn about meeting people at their point of deepest need, the stronger our commitment and service to Christ becomes. We are convinced it is in serving Christ and our fellow man that we live our relationship with Him in a way that pleases and glorifies Him.

Chapter Two
Love God, Love Y'all, That's All

I recently shared with a good friend my need to hear the words of Jesus, in a simple, straightforward way. It's difficult to live a Christian life in a simple, straightforward way; we live in a broken world; it's a sad commentary to watch the news and see the levels of division, hate and lack of civil discourse. I travel to scripture to help me understand and deal with the brokenness and keep me focused on Critical Presence.

I think most of us have our favorite scripture. When we first discovered it, we learned it, discerned it and embraced it. I've learned that it doesn't stop there—as time goes by we draw deeper meaning as it comforts us, teaches us, guides us. That's the way it is with God's Word and we glorify Him for that!

"Love the Lord God with all your heart, and with all your soul, and with all your heart. This is the first and greatest commandment. And the second is like it: Love your neighbor as yourself. All the Law and the Prophets hang on these two commandments." —Mt. 22:37-40 That's my favorite scripture.

Living and serving in this world with its lack of civil discourse, division, prejudice and hate and trying to separate the good from the evil is difficult at best and judgement of my neighbor is above my pay grade. Standing for my moral compass is easy, personal and without prejudice to any person or group.

Love Him, Love Y'all, That's All—simple and easy for anyone to understand. Following His great commandments lead me to Servant Ministry. *"Just as the Son of Man came not to be served but to serve and to give his life as a ransom for many."* —Mt. 20:28 Jesus calls us to follow Him into Critical

Bro. Vance Moore

Presence—meeting our fellow man at their point of deepest need. **He Knew I'd Need His Wisdom. Thank You Jesus!**
Love Him, Love All Y'all—That's All. It's liberating.

My Epiphany

These thoughts are based on a book by Rev. Adam Hamilton called *Half-Truths*. The material is about common sayings that are often associated with Christianity and said by many Christians. And at first, they may sound OK, and we often mean well when we say them. But when we look a little closer, we realize that these sayings aren't as true or as Christian as we first might have thought. The final saying we are looking at today is "Love the sinner. Hate the sin."

As I watch the news, local or national and as I engage folks in everyday conversation I am saddened by words and actions filled with hatred and discord where there should be love and civil discourse. Make no mistake in my remarks. When people are killed and injured by an act of domestic terrorism for the world to see on TV, the church should not remain silent. When words filled with hatred and civility are the order of the day there is a need for the Word of God to be heard.

I was unsure that I could come up with the words needed to theologically address the events taking place throughout our country. Like many of you, I am still trying to make sense of what has taken place, and how God is calling us to actively engage in opposition to hate and division happening in society today. We need to be talking about love. We need to be talking about sin. We need to be talking about hate. And it's more important than ever that we speak loudly of love and tread carefully when talking about hate, sin and sinners.

Love the sinner. Hate the sin. It sounds okay, on first read. How can it be bad to love anybody? And doesn't it sound really Christ-like to love sinners? And shouldn't we hate sin? Especially if we think of sin as things that we do that hurt

Critical Presence: Love God, Love Y'all, That's All

ourselves, others, or hurt God.

The phrase is not in the Bible, though. It is thought to have originated with St. Augustine several hundred years after Jesus. In one of his letters he called for early Christians to have a "love for mankind and a hatred of sins." Over the ages, this saying has appeared in various forms, but they all mean basically the same thing. If we know of someone who is sinning, we should continue to love them as a sinner, but hate and condemn the sinful actions they do. And this does sound true, right?

Never stop loving someone no matter what horrible things they've done. But here's the catch. Rarely, are we ever able to contain our hatred only to the sin.

Ghandi once spoke about this saying: *"Hate the sin and not the sinner is a precept which, though easy enough to understand, is rarely practiced, and that is why the poison of hatred spreads in the world."*

Love the sinner. Hate the sin. If we practice this, we end up focusing much more on sin and the label of sinner, much more than we focus on love. **Jesus never said love the sinner. Jesus said love your neighbor. Jesus knew that if he commanded people to love the sinner, they would begin looking people more as sinners than neighbor.**

Think about it. If I said to you right now, I want you to love everyone sitting here in the congregation today, especially those who have been recently diagnosed with a highly contagious form of smallpox. Are you going to focus on loving your neighbor, or on who looks a little under the weather today?

Love the sinner. Hate the sin, doesn't lead us to love, instead it leads us immediately to a place of judging who is a sinner and what sins are they guilty of. Love the sinner. Hate the sin, is often used as code for saying "I judge you. You are a sinner, you should be ashamed that you do, but even though I am better than you, I will love you anyway."

This is a good time to read our second scripture. Because it addresses this very topic.

"He also told this parable to some who trusted in themselves that they were righteous and regarded others with contempt: 'Two men went up to the temple to pray, one a Pharisee and the other a tax-collector. The Pharisee, standing by himself, was praying thus, "God, I thank you that I am not like other people: thieves, rogues, adulterers, or even like this tax-collector. I fast twice a week; I give a tenth of all my income." But the tax-collector, standing far off, would not even look up to heaven, but was beating his breast and saying, "God, be merciful to me, a sinner!" I tell you, this man went down to his home justified rather than the other; for all who exalt themselves will be humbled, but all who humble themselves will be exalted.'"
—Luke 18:9-14

In Jesus day, the Pharisees were Jewish authorities who, by all accounts, should be considered as righteous. They strictly lived their lives according to proper Jewish laws. And, to many who first heard Jesus tell this story, they would probably agree with the Pharisee's self-assessment. He was a righteous man, especially when compared with the tax-collector. The tax-collector would have even agreed that the Pharisee was more righteous than he was.

<u>But in a twist at the end of the story it is the tax collector who is justified by God, and not the righteous Pharisee.</u>

Here is the essential contrast. One makes a claim to righteousness based on his own accomplishments, while the other relies entirely upon the Lord's benevolence. Rather than be grateful for his blessings, the Pharisee appears smug to the point of despising others. In his mind there are two kinds of people: the righteous and the immoral, and he is grateful that he has placed himself among the righteous. The tax collector, on the other hand, isn't so much humble as desperate. He is too overwhelmed

Critical Presence: Love God, Love Y'all, That's All

by his plight to take time to divide humanity into sides. All he recognizes as he stands near the Temple is his own great need. He therefore stakes his hopes and claims not on anything he has done or deserved but entirely on the mercy of God.

What matters to God in this story, and in our own lives, is not who is righteous, but who is judgmental and who is not. Not who lives a so-called perfect life, but who realizes their dependence on God and that righteousness is a gift from God and not our own doing.

So coming back to Love the sinner. Hate the sin. The problem with this saying is that it focuses us on the sins of others, on judgment of others, rather than on our own sin and being honest about where we are with God. Love the Sinner. Hate the sin, at its heart focuses on the sins of others and our judgment of them.

In the *Half-Truths* book, Adam Hamilton tells this story about Billy Graham:

Some time ago I read an interview with Billy Graham's eldest daughter, Gigi. She was her father's date to Time magazine's seventy-fifth anniversary party, a banquet in Washington, DC. President Bill Clinton spoke at the event. He had just been impeached by the House of Representatives for perjury and obstruction of justice. The charge of perjury involved what President Clinton had said, under oath, about his relationship with White House intern Monica Lewinsky. At the banquet, her father sat with President and Mrs. Clinton. He was warm and gracious to them. After the dinner ended and Graham and Gigi were riding back to their hotel, the two discussed difficulties the president and First Lady were going through with so many people gossiping and judging. Gigi said her father's simple comment was, *"It's the Holy Spirit's job to convict; it's God's job to judge; and it's our job to love."*

It is our job to love. Not to judge. It is our job to love.

Bro. Vance Moore

When we label someone as sinner, we stop seeing the person and we start seeing the sin. *Our job is not to convict but to love.*

Should we keep silent about the problem of sin? Of course not. There are absolutely times when Christians must stand up and name sin and evil for what it is. This moment in the life of our country is one of those times. We must name hatred, racism, white supremacy, and the failure to condemn them as sin. Any Christian who engages in actions or rhetoric motivated by hate or racism, has ceased to represent Christ. Any Christian who remains silent in the face of racism and hatred, will have to answer to God for their complicity.

Here's the slippery slope; in our rush to eliminate prejudice we must be careful not to disadvantage one individual or group in order to heal another group. We must be careful not to place anyone into a group because of their race, age, gender, religion. Jesus did not come to save skin color or participate in any other human action that endorses favoritism. He came to save souls and all souls are equal.

Want to participate in a God Thang with me? Here 'tis—I have been struggling, trying to find some meaningful illustration that would share with you how strongly I feel about Love God, Love Y'all, That's All. I turned on the 6 o'clock news and the next news report made me sit up, pay attention and say out loud, "Thank You Jesus." Here's my take on this news report:

Background: About a year ago a female white police officer, off duty, entered an unlocked apartment. Her testimony was that she mistakenly thought it was her apartment. Inside was the tenant, a 28-year-old African American male. She shot and killed him. She recently went on trial in Dallas for that killing. She was charged with murder and the jury had choices to convict of murder, manslaughter or acquit.

She was convicted of murder and sentenced to ten years in

Critical Presence: Love God, Love Y'all, That's All

prison. Depending on your understanding of this news account, there are multiple issues involved, murder, police, race—you see what I mean. What I witnessed next was simply Jesus letting me see how it should be done. At the sentencing the family had the opportunity always afforded to families of the victims. I want to share the story of one of those family members. 18-year-old Brandt, the victim's brother, asked the judge for permission to hug the woman, and after receiving permission from the judge, left the witness box and hugged the woman just convicted of killing his brother, expressed his forgiveness and shared with her that God would forgive her. Later on, the judge gave her a Bible and told her that would be a good place to begin. What did I just witness—Love God, Love Y'all, That's It—you betcha. I saw a Christian man loving God by forgiving the woman that killed his brother. Period, no racism, no cop bashing, no hate, just a Christian doing what Jesus told him to do Love God, Love your neighbor—and then I saw the judge that just sentenced her to 10 years in prison because she was guilty of taking a life, leave the bench, and bring God's Word to her. Talk about Christian values. The judge had the responsibility to apply man's law, she's a judge; She showed her responsibility as a Christian when she literally took the Word of God to someone judged and sentenced and gave her that beginning point to forgiveness and restoration in God.

    I sat back and asked myself, "How in the world could I do this? This event tells the whole story. This is where the rubber meets the road. Now we're in the action phase of our beliefs— The words to an old song came almost immediately to my mind. Thought I might share them with you!

> When we walk with the Lord
> In the light of His Word,
> What a glory He sheds on our way;
> While we do His good will,

Bro. Vance Moore

He abides with us still,
And with all who will trust and obey.

> Trust and obey,
> For there's no other way
> To be happy in Jesus,
> But to trust and obey.

Not a shadow can rise,
Not a cloud in the skies,
But His smile quickly drives it away;
Not a doubt or a fear,
Not a sigh or a tear,
Can abide while we trust and obey.

Not a burden we bear,
Not a sorrow we share,
But our toil He doth richly repay;
Not a grief or a loss,
Not a frown or a cross,
But is blest if we trust and obey.

But we never can prove
The delights of His love,
Until all on the altar we lay;
For the favor He shows,
And the joy He bestows,
Are for them who will trust and obey.

Then in fellowship sweet
We will sit at His feet,
Or we'll walk by His side in the way;
What He says we will do;
Where He sends, we will go,
Never fear, only trust and obey. —John Sammis, 1887

Combine the words of this Trust and Obey song with that simple command to Love. Maybe, just maybe Jesus has

Critical Presence: Love God, Love Y'all, That's All

already touched this need! Maybe, just maybe John Sammis got it right!!

We must resist the urge to judge others and label simply as sinners or to think of them as lesser people, not as holy and righteous as we are. Our job is not to convict but to love. **The truth in "Love the sinner, hate the sin" stops with the first word: Love.**

When we use this saying, we are first and foremost defining that person as a sinner, rather than as someone we love. Furthermore, as we read from Matthew, we should not be judging other people, we have enough sin in our own lives that makes us liable to judgement. The only person we should label as sinner is ourselves. Love the sinner, hate the sin should be rewritten and we should instead be saying, I love you, even despite the fact that I am a sinner.

- Everything happens for a reason.
- God helps those who help themselves.
- God won't give you more than you can handle.
- God said it. I believe it. That settles it.
- Love the sinner. Hate the sin.

Five half-truths. If there is some truth to these why do we really need to be worried about saying these things? If we mean well, isn't that enough. Unfortunately, that's not enough. The reality is these half-truths can hurt people who need hope and healing. These half-truths can be destructive to someone in a time of need. These half-truths can discourage people and turn people away from God and Christianity.

And even more importantly, why would we give someone a half-truth when we could give them the whole truth of a God who loves them and is there to support and guide them every step of the way.

I am indebted to Rev. Adam Hamilton and his book *Half Truths* for the basis of these thoughts.

I'd like remind you of the "whole truths" we found behind the half-truths we have rejected. We reject the idea that everything that happens is God's will. Instead we say that whatever happens, God is able to able to work through it, to redeem it, and to bring good from it.

We reject the idea that God only helps those who help themselves. We recognize that God expects us to do what we can to help ourselves. We pray and we work. But ultimately the very definition of grace and mercy is that God helps those who cannot help themselves.

We reject the idea that God won't give us more than we can handle. This is partly because we reject the idea that whatever adversity we face is given to us by God. What we do believe is that God will help us handle all the adversity life will give us.

We reject the idea that every verse of Scripture should be read, out of context, as the literal words of God. Instead we recognize that the biblical authors were people, influenced by God but not merely stenographers. Like all of us they were shaped by, and responded to, the historical circumstances in which they lived. And thus we believe that, when they are rightly interpreted, God speaks through the words of Scripture in order to teach, guide, shape and encourage us.

Finally, we reject the notion that God calls upon Christians to "love the sinner, hate the sin." When we choose to focus on the sins of others and speak of hating their sin, we violate the words and spirit of Jesus. Paul calls us to hate our sins, and Jesus calls us to love our neighbors, all of whom are sinners. When we demonstrate love and not judgment, we draw people to Christ rather than repel them from him.

Liberation

Allow me to share a story to help you see the liberation: ask yourself, is this story about Critical Presence, meeting people at their point of deepest need? OR is it about Matthew 22:37-40, Love God, Love Y'all, That's All!

Critical Presence: Love God, Love Y'all, That's All

One of the most moving illustrations of the fruits of the Spirit and of God using our gifts wherever we are, in whatever condition we are in is through a story shared with me by Doris Taylor. Doris shares this story:

Meet My Niece and the Whistler

I was inspired today by a friend who has had to face many battles in her life but always has an inspirational word regardless the conditions and circumstances she faces or has faced. This friend made me think of an incident I worked several years ago on my job as a paramedic. God moves in mysterious ways, but He always gives us what we need, not always what we WANT.

A call came in the 911 dispatch one morning in July about a man lying on the side of the road and a church bus of teenagers on a church trip found him. They stopped and realized the man was clutching his chest and asking for help. One of these children called 911, and my unit responded. My partner and I knew heat advisories were issued that morning and it was already spiking 100° before 10 a.m.

As we arrived on scene, a mid-sized man lay in a fetal position surrounded by all the teenagers who stopped to help. They were very polite and told me of their findings when they stopped. Which in this day and time is brave love for another human, because his condition might not have not been legitimate.

As I assessed this what appeared to be mid 60's gentleman, I realized he was having a heart attack: high blood pressure, excruciating chest pain described as a "squeezing heaviness." I placed my monitor on him as quickly as I could and needed to cool him down as he had layers of filthy clothes on despite the extreme heat. The pores on his skin were full of black dirt. His hands were swollen and looked as if he were a

Bro. Vance Moore

diesel mechanic who had just gotten off work. My monitor showed just what I suspected, ST elevations in what we call "tombstoning." It really resembles a fireman's a hat. This was an MI in progress.

Uncertain of the outcome or even how long this had been going on, I transported this man in emergency status. We also had no medical history on him, as he had not seen a physician in over thirty-five years since his discharge from military service (He had served our country as a soldier, doing two tours of duty in Vietnam).

As I administered medications going down the road in the back of that ambulance, I looked at him real hard and tried to figure out why anyone in the world who loved any member of their family would allow a person to live like this: on the road, homeless, zero contacts and penniless. I continued on with my job to save him and preserve life, but my heart filled with pity. We arrived at the hospital and all my findings about his physical condition were confirmed.

The next issue was that we didn't have the services of a cardiovascular surgeon. This patient had to be transported elsewhere. I realize this could be an even greater problem. I recognized how difficult it is in this day for a patient to get accepted into a larger, more specialized facility when he has no job, no insurance and lives in a tent on the side of the road. To be sure, this is sad, ain't it? But our great Emergency Physician that day succeeded and I had the privilege—and I do mean privilege—of transporting this man over a hundred miles down the road where he could receive the help he needed.

And now the story gets really interesting part. This gentleman was well-known in these parts, in that he had been traveling from east to west coast for nearly forty years, always camping in the same locations along his way. But this time he told me he was trying to get to Missouri, where they have a home for vets with medical problems, a place where he would

Critical Presence: Love God, Love Y'all, That's All

be accepted and he knew really needed help. He was crying as he told me he knew his time was near.

Of course, me being me, I had to say something off color and make him smile. Then we chimed into a detailed conversation of his life. I ask him why he chose this way of living: waiting on a handout, no shelter from the heat, cold, rain? He informed me he had a tent, and said it proudly. I just grinned.

He told me that he came home after his tours and found his mom had lost a battle of cancer in California where they lived. Six months later his father died of a stroke and, one year after, that his only sibling—a sister—also left this world, losing her battle to cancer. He had lost everything, right down to the last stick of furniture, trying to pay medical bills off. And when he failed, he ended up homeless, without anything, anybody, anywhere. But he was smiling the whole time he was telling me these things and of his book he was writing about the serial killers he had actually met and had dinner with on his travels and all the things he had seen and done.

Then he teared up again and I asked him was he in pain? He stated no, the morphine was helping his chest pain, but his heart was broken. He revealed to me that everything he owned was at certain place on the side of the interstate inside his tent in the opposite direction we were going. EVEN his notebook he was writing his book in. Also in that tent he said he had a small am/fm radio and an ashtray. He stated the book was very important to him and his tent as he had had it for many years and now he said, "Even that's gone."

He had a small dusty bag with him and he reached into it and pulled out the most beautiful crochet pineapple doily as big as the hood of that ambulance. He offered it to me for being so kind to him and listening. He said he made them and traded them for food and necessity. As he pulled out four more huge doilies, I offered to buy all of them, as I knew he would need a couple days in a motel room to recoup after his surgery or the elements outside would finish him off. He told me, if I would accept a certain one as a gift, he would sell me the others with the caveat that I could do a small favor for him.

"Will you see if someone can help salvage my tent and my radio. I'm sure the animals have gotten the food that was in there by now, but ask them to get my notebook."

WHAT WAS I GONNA SAY? DO? WHAT WOULD YOU SAY? DO?

I assured him it would be taken care of as soon as I returned from this transfer with him, that I would personally see to it that his belongings were safe until his return. As I dropped him off at the receiving facility, he said something to me that I'll never forget. Maybe that's what drove me to do all I did for him. He said, "You know the only difference between you and me, ma'am?" I said, "I'm a woman and you're a man?" I laughed as I winked.

He chuckled and said, "Besides that?"

I said, "No sir. I don't reckon I do."

He said, "A paycheck. That's really the only thing that separates us all."

It made sense to me.

Again he told me where to look and with a little help from people who lived nearby where he stayed each time he passed through, we found his tent, book, radio and ashtray. The animals indeed had eaten all his food, except for the five-day-old chicken legs he still had in his backpack when I dropped him off with it at the hospital. I bundled it all up for him, wondering if he would even return to claim it at all. I gave him my phone number—stupid you probably think, but I had to do it so he would have hope he could return for his only belongings in this world and that they were safe. Those generous people who searched the woods with me that evening for these treasures of his told me they called him "the Whistler."

Of course I was curious as to how he got that name. They

Critical Presence: Love God, Love Y'all, That's All

informed me that for years during the months of summer he always had camped there and as the sun set each evening he would whistle. It sounded just like a train coming. I read his writings and I must admit he was not kidding about his adventures. There were dates that coincided with dates of the areas these convicted killers were arrested. It made chills run up my spine.

Three days later a social worker called my phone and informed me he had the surgery and was being discharged. He gave her my number after telling her about this paramedic that was seeing after his things. She told me they were providing the over 100-mile transport back, but could not just drop him off on the side of the road because of the liability they would face—something of which I was quite aware. So they were transporting him back to our facility's parking lot.

I was at home that day, so I immediately gathered his bundle-of-life up, carried it to the hospital ambulance bay and dropped it off for him to pick up as I told the social worker I would do. As I drove to drop his things off, I thought, he needs more money and some enforcing words to make him understand he needed to rest comfortably somewhere before he continued his journey to Missouri. So I wrote him a letter. Because I've already shared so much, I'll not share the details, but I will say I also left him some money to care for himself within his notebook. My heart felt heavy. While I felt blessed to have met this man and wanted to help him more, I knew it was better not get to attached. That's why I'm a medic, I don't like getting attached.

My friends at work the next day stated he retrieved his things, thanked everyone for their help and disappeared after asking about me. I've driven by there at sunset several times in the summer months at sunset, but I've never heard "the Whistler."

I pray he made it to Missouri. I hope he becomes a renowned author. I pray he found somebody to belong to and

Bro. Vance Moore

he could claim for his own. But most of all, I pray he didn't die alone, cold and the animals stealing his food.
  God bless you, "Whistler."

Chapter Three
Critical Presence Beginnings

My ministry had its' beginnings in the 1990's. Back then I had never heard the term Critical Presence or meeting people at their point of deepest need. What I did have was a sense that someone needed to help the men (and yes a few women as well) that we passed on the side of the roads around Little Rock.

At that time I was Elder Chair at First Christian Church of Sherwood, a community in the greater Little Rock area. Harvey Johnston, my brother-in-law had gotten me involved in the food pantry and working there half day a week exposed me to the less fortunate in our local community. Problem was, the homeless I was seeing on the side of the highways never found the food pantries. You would see them pan handling but not at the food pantries.

I started a ministry we called YANA, an acrostic meaning You Are Not Alone. YANA quickly became a ministry, one of several the church supported. We all pitched in, bought items that could be placed in a brown paper bag and carried in our cars and trucks. Back then, we didn't see any other "blessing bag" ministries in our local area. We would keep the brown bags in the toolbox of the truck; when we saw a homeless person on the side of the road, I'd stop and ask the homeless person if he or she was hungry. I made it a point to not "preach" to him, but would ask if they wanted me to say a prayer for them. Almost always the prayer would follow and end with a blessing. I'd like to share a special story with you from the YANA days.

Bro. Vance Moore

I SAW JESUS TODAY

In the early days of my ministry I worked a full-time construction job and did ministry along the way. YANA was the outreach arm of that ministry. Work carried me all around town and much of it on the interstates. Little Rock seemed to be a magnet for the homeless traveling thru central Arkansas. Many days we would meet five or six homeless folk.

On this particular day I was busy, real busy. My wife, Jeannie and I were on our way to one of the jobs I was working on. I was pushing to finish the job. While I loved the YANA ministry, I also had to make a living.

We were coming off the interstate exit ramp and I could see the young man and a little dog on the entry ramp across the turn lane I was in; I turned left thinking I just didn't have the time to stop. I didn't want to stop, I was busy, real busy.

As I made the turn Jeannie said, "You need to help that guy."

My heart knew she was right, I just didn't want too. I knew it wouldn't do to resist Jeannie or God. I pulled into the left turn lane, got back on the interstate going back the other way to the last exit so I could U turn and retrace my steps. Four miles later, two up and two back, I'm on the exit ramp in the right lane.

As I pulled forward onto the onramp, I saw a young man and his little dog. I confess that I was put off by the ear studs in both ears. Probably five or six in each ear. Just for a moment I felt a sense of judging someone unfairly. He did not fit the profile of the people I wanted to help.

I pulled off, went to my toolbox and retrieved a brown blessing bag. As I walked towards him something happened I will never forget. As my eyes made contact with him and I spoke the words I always said in these times, "Hey Bro, you hungry?"

In that moment, that microsecond in time, I had a sense

Critical Presence: Love God, Love Y'all, That's All

come over me; down south we call it "chilli bumps." Whatever you want to call it, I knew I looked into the eyes of Jesus. I shared the YANA bag with him and said a prayer for him. He'll probably never know what a profound impact he made on me. Sharing this story with you, 25+ years later, I have a sense, tears and chilli bumps.

Thank You Jesus for giving me a glimpse that day. A glimpse of the blessing when we encounter Jesus by meeting people at their point of deepest need and answering the call to serve that need. Oh, and by the way, another lesson; Satan is always trying to inject prejudice and judgment when we doing Gods' work. *"Submit yourselves, then, to God. Resist the devil, and he will flee from you."*—James 4;7

Bro. Vance Moore

Chapter Four
Westside Story

All of us have those rare moments in our lives that are unforgettable. In my ministry, I have been blessed with many, many wonderful, indelible memories. The five years after Hurricane Katrina that I spent in New Orleans, Louisiana, building the Westside Mission Center and serving as its director is full of those memories. From the very beginning it was obvious to me, as to the thousands of volunteers who served and those received their service that this experience was something far bigger than any of us. It was historically and spiritually momentous. I called it a "God Thang."

Westside Mission Center Poster

Critical Presence: Love God, Love Y'all, That's All

Critical Presence: It's a God Thang was later published to tell the story of the victims of Hurricane Katrina and of the volunteers who came to serve them in their time of deepest need. The book told the story of four distinct groups of people: The first and largest group was the people impacted by Hurricane Katrina, literally hundreds of thousands of people not only in New Orleans but throughout the Gulf Coast and reaching inward for hundreds of miles. Before going to New Orleans to start the Westside Mission Center, I thought this is the only group involved. How very wrong I was.

The second cluster is actually a subgroup for the first: Westside Christian Church, or rather what remained of Westside as a congregation.

The third group in the story is the volunteers: several thousand volunteers over a period of five years.

Who is the fourth group? I am the fourth group. I call myself "a group" because this story encompassed not only the time spent at the Mission Center in New Orleans, but my ministry from the moment I stepped into New Orleans going forward as long my Lord allows me to serve.

The first group, the people of New Orleans, were the intended recipients of our efforts through the larger regional church, the Great River Region. Our region intended to reach into New Orleans, building Mission Center, to minister to the members of the church, and to make a positive impact on the local area. We had no idea of the scope of the task upon which we were embarking.

My recollection of the names of all those people we helped is limited, though I will mention a few of them below. Ironically, while I might not remember all their names, burned in my memory forever are their faces, especially their eyes. I see them clearly in my memory. I see the desperation in their eyes. I see what I have often described has that "lost look."

In fact the expression they wore was a little bit more

complicated than one of simply being lost. In the beginning it was a look of distrust. Over time I came to recognize that their psyche had been devastated by the trauma and pain they had suffered. This was the source of that lost look. They needed something and someone to rekindle the hope they so desperately needed. One of the greatest blessings that we as volunteers and I as an individual received throughout this process

My Brother Howard

My life was forever impacted by an older black man, Pastor Howard Washington. Howard is with Jesus now. If there was ever a "race well run," it was the life of Howard Washington. His story is well-known to the thousands of volunteers, to the hundreds and hundreds of people in the Lower 9th Ward of New Orleans who were touched by his walk with Christ. I doubt seriously that Howard ever heard the phrase "Critical Presence" and if he did, he would not have been able to define it in theological terms. However no one I've ever met had a fuller grasp and a better working knowledge of this thing we call Critical Presence.

Long after my time at Westside Mission Center came to a close, I was invited back to participate in what is a grand tradition in African-American churches. Pastor Appreciation Day is a special event during which the local church and the community celebrate their pastor. I was asked to be the keynote speaker for that event at Pastor Washington's congregation, Greater Jerusalem Church. As I sat waiting to speak, I listened in awe as countless people rose and gave their personal testimony about this man.

An older woman stood. She was nervous. Her voice was quivering. She told the group that she had needed a prescription filled, but she had no money. She said, "I went to see Pastor. He got my prescription. He knowed that I have to have my prescription." Finding the money to purchase her medicine might have been a little thing to a lot of people. To her, though, it was a lifeline. Pastor was there at her point of deepest need. That is the perfect example of Critical Presence.

Howard and the Muslim

Howard had a man stop by his place one day. He was a cab driver. I don't remember his name. His story is told in the first book, *Critical Presence: It's a God Thang*. What I do remember is it he is from a different faith background than Howard and I. He was a Muslim. That's relevant for a couple reasons: one was his statement to Pastor Washington that he was a Muslim and he needed help. Howard told me the man was a Muslim. I want my readers to be sure I understood that. Nonetheless, the man needed help and we needed to help him. This is a neat, essential lesson, Critical Presence has no a filter to weed out people who aren't like us. Bias is outside of its boundaries. At that time, he was the only Muslim I had ever encountered. I learned quickly that they are very private people. At least this fellow was. He needed us to help him with his house, but he also needed to work every day at his job. This created a dilemma. Who was going to be at the house while the workers were here? What a sacrifice it was for him when he handed me a key. He had to trust someone from a different culture and a different religious background to help him in his time of deepest need. Once again, Critical Presence touched the lives of everyone involved—the one in need and those who set aside all differences to help.

Gwen as Served and Servant

I think it's fitting, as we reflect on the crossroads of talent and need, to hear the story of someone who experienced

Bro. Vance Moore

Critical Presence both from the perspective of the person in need, and also from the perspective of the mission worker—my wife Gwen:

Gwen Moore

Before Hurricane Katrina I had lived in New Orleans for forty-five years. Jerry, my husband, of forty years, had gone to be with the Lord. We had raised two daughters, both of whom resided in the New Orleans area at the time of Hurricane Katrina. I was a member of Chalmette Baptist Church. I attended regularly and participated in most church activities. I was supportive of different outreaches that the church did; I recall helping to make fruit baskets and other of outreach. My memory is of Chalmette is of being a contented and happy member for my local church. That is to say, I had a good faith life and was comfortable in my church before Hurricane Katrina.

After Katrina my world changed dramatically. Like thousands of other people in the New Orleans and the Gulf Coast Area, I lost everything. I had no insurance. I had no

Critical Presence: Love God, Love Y'all, That's All

savings. I was now dependent upon other people and FEMA. I was blessed by having another faith community, First Baptist Church in D'Lo, Mississippi. This was where my faith changed dramatically. Before Hurricane Katrina my faith was solid, but as with most long-time members of the Christian churches it was just a normal part of life. After Hurricane Katrina, suddenly I had nothing but my faith. I knew hanging on to my faith in our Lord would bring me thru. Seeing that faith in action is the true life-changing part of what happened to me.

The people of the church at D'Lo opened their hearts and they helped me in many ways. They help me find a place to live, they bought me furniture, they help me find clothes, they help me find the basic necessities of life that, until then, I had always provided for myself. I became part of their church family. I quickly became a part of their family of God. I was blessed when they involved me in their mission efforts in Pearlington Mississippi. I felt like I could give a good perspective of what had happened to me and share it with the people of Pearlington while we were working on their houses. It was a time of service, of seeing faith in action, and of being able to give back in some small way.

During the period of time between Hurricane Katrina and meeting Brother Vance, I experienced day-to-day life around the ministers of the church. My brother-in-law was the pastor of First Baptist Church in D'Lo. We did lots of outreach and I was blessed to be involved in much of that. I had never been that close to disaster, and I definitely had never been that close to reaching out to people who had lost everything. Knowing that ministers do good things is one thing; seeing them giving of themselves on a day-to-day basis is heartwarming and it touches you deep in your soul.

In 2008 I met brother Vance at Westside Mission Center in New Orleans. I was visiting with one of my friends who still lived in New Orleans after Hurricane Katrina. Vance and I

Bro. Vance Moore

had both lost our spouses, my Jerry in 2003, and his Jeannie in 2007. Over the next year we became friends, never thinking that we would become life partners. We married in February, 2010. Immediately my life changed radically.

My brother-in-law was a pastor and I had been around him and his wife, my sister, for many years. But I had no idea what it meant to be married to a pastor. And suddenly the man I was married to is a pastor who directs the rebuilding of homes and lives in the town that I had called home for all those years. I was able to see and experience volunteers coming from all over United States to the Westside Mission Center to serve God. I found being a pastor's wife to be somewhat strange at first. It was somewhat like moving from the outside to the inside. I had done mission work and it was meaningful and a blessing to me.

Now, though, I was married to someone who was working many, many hours, rebuilding lives. In the beginning it was overwhelming to a degree. I understood what it meant when I heard Brother Vance say we meet people at their point of deepest need. I had been one of those people. I had received at my point of deepest need. And now I was a part of the team that was serving those needs. To say that I was totally comfortable—no. It was daunting, and a little bit scary. We saw and ministered to so much need. We felt so much obligation.

I had made a decision after Hurricane Katrina to retire. I had become comfortable. To say that changed me would be an understatement. I have changed so much over the last eight years. I have always been a people person. I have always loved my fellow man. It has taken more than eight years to begin to understand what it means to be a pastor's wife. I don't mind saying it changed me. I've learned that our Lord gives us strength and resources when we need them most.

Gwen is a living example of the astonishing transformations through Critical Presence. She is a constant reminder to me of the power of Christ and God's ability to empower and change us precisely at the most crucial instances of our lives.

In 2010 we closed the mission. I became full time Regional Pastor, a position I held along with being the Director of Westside Mission Center since 2009. I traveled the entirety of the Great River Region for the next two years. I was asked as well to work with our mission effort to the *Iglesia* churches in the Dominican Republic. I went there and I experienced the same desire on the part of those congregations to reach out in faithful mission. In a part of the world where poverty and hardship are the order of the day, I saw amazing generosity and compassion in the name of Jesus Christ. Throughout my experience as Regional Pastor, or traveling throughout our nation or in the Dominican Republic, my experience taught me that those churches which were growing were the churches that were invested in volunteers and mission.

Westside Volunteers

A multitude of my memories of the volunteers involve young people. Just to see their parents and their churches bring them to New Orleans in order to teach them to share the love of Christ was an overwhelming blessing. Many of them seemed to experience their work at the mission center as being a sort of unique, neat and extraordinary vacation. As I interacted with them, I realized they could be over on the beach in Mississippi or Florida having a great time during their summer break. Yet there they were, at Westside Mission Center—as one of the parents of the kids expressed it— "Doing things in the Lower Ninth Ward to help people: getting dirty, nasty, sweaty, doing extremely hard work, and I can't even get them to clean up their room at home." I was often told that kind of story.

Bro. Vance Moore

I remember once, as we were doing our "where did you see God today" session, having a teenager say to me, "Brother Vance, we don't want to hear about Jesus. We want to do Jesus." What a clear and concise definition of meeting people at their point of deepest need, an awesome definition of Critical Presence. They were saying, "You told us about Jesus and we've chosen to embody his love. We are staying here to serve as he served. Now let us go do what Jesus is calling us to do."

My Story

The final group is made up of Bro. Vance and his ministry. Before Katrina I was the pastor of a local church in Benton, Arkansas. My late wife Jeannie and I had been dealing with cancer for several years—she with the disease, and I as the caretaker. Although the medical issue we faced carried a real degree of difficulty, our ministry and church life was good.

During that time, my ministry outreach consisted of varying degrees of working with homeless people. Several years prior I had started an outreach mission called YANA, and an acronym for You Are Not Alone. Providing blessing bags of emergency food, working with local homeless groups—this was the essence of that part of my ministry. I found it tremendously satisfying and that work continues today as part of the outreach of my ministry at Central Christian Church.

Looking back on that period of my ministry, I thought I had a good grasp of what it meant to be a pastor, a minister to my flock and virtuous Christian. In early 2006, the Great River Region commissioned Jeannie and me as missionaries to New Orleans. In that service Barb Jones expressed that we would be "in-country missionaries" but truly we were missionaries. Little did I know how much the decision to move to New Orleans and our missionary commission would change my life

Critical Presence: Love God, Love Y'all, That's All

and my ministry. Yes, I had traveled to New Orleans, talked to the members at Westside Christian Church and even formulated the plan of our mission with Barb before this commissioning. Yet from the moment I set foot in New Orleans everything changed.

From the time of my arrival forward, all-day, every-day was filled with the mission work of ministry: ministry to Westside Christian Church, ministry to the volunteers, ministry to the people of New Orleans, and the ministry of caring for Jeannie until she be went to be with Jesus in July 2007.

As I lived through those days, so often I thought of the way that, in sermons and in conversation with other Christians, we talk about leaning on Christ. Quickly I learned that I could not accomplish these demanding tasks on my own. I learned right away I had to depend on him. He came to me in so many different ways. Sometimes I would see him in the volunteers. Sometimes I would see him in the people of New Orleans. Often I would encounter him in an individual. First I would see his presence in the eyes. It is so true—the eyes are the mirror of the soul. Then I hear that person's story. It was always about a need, always about the deepest need at the time. Sometimes it was a need of help to rebuild. Sometimes it was a volunteer expressing an irresistible need to help. Many, many times it was, "This is where I saw God today."

This brought to my mind the magnificent Psalm 139, in which King David said he could go nowhere without encountering God. That's how I felt. I'm not sure that, at the time I was going through those experiences, I realized how much I truly needed him. One thing I was sure of, though: every time I needed something, it was provided. And as I would live through that particular challenge, whatever it was, I knew it was only through Jesus that we were able to accomplish the work set before us. I have been blessed with a certain degree of humility. In retrospect, that seems almost laughable to me. As I look at my life, I realize that humility has become a necessity. It is a living reality. When I realize there is absolutely no way I could have accomplished all these miraculous stuff on my own, it grounds me, humbles me and fills me with gratitude that Christ is using me to accomplish his work.

Our work in New Orleans was also a tremendous educational experience. I had to learn so many things at Westside Mission Center. I saw devastation and need at the local community and at the property owner level that defies description. I saw people beaten down—all the way down. I saw those same people experience the love of Christ through volunteers. I saw their hearts begin to warm. I saw love: brotherly love; agape love; the love that is embodied in Critical Presence. I learned so much more about what it means to be a minister. I learned what it means to serve. I learned what Christ meant when he said, "I came not to be served but to serve."

On July 3rd, 2007, Jeannie went to be with the Lord. I'll always remember that morning, 3:26 a.m., sitting by her bedside in the partially completed parsonage. I remember talking to God. Not long before this night, Jeannie had told me she was going to go and be with Jesus and that I could come too if I wanted. I knew she was heavily medicated, but I understood her message. So that night I said to God, "If you're ready for me, I'm ready to go. I only ask that, if you leave me here, let me serve You and let me make it count."

I continued on at Westside Mission Center for another three years. Then I served three years as Regional Pastor for the Great River Region. Today I am at Central Christian Church in Hattiesburg Mississippi, as a local pastor. I pray daily that I am living up to my promise to make it count for Jesus.

Two years after Jeannie went to be with Jesus, God sent Gwen to me. We've been married now for ten years and we serve the Lord together. God has truly blessed me.

Chapter Five
Critical Presence Today

Wayne Scott

Wayne Scott was born 12/22/1948. We would consider Wayne a relic of some sort. Born and raised on a farm north of Petal, Mississippi, Wayne attended vocational training in diesel mechanics at the age of 16. Early on he injured his back and that ended his diesel mechanic school. He went to work for a local family as a farm hand around 1965 and continues in semi-retirement in 2020; fifty-four years working for the Rayburn family as a farm hand and general worker for the family. The Rayburn children have grown up knowing him as "Uncle Wayne" even though there is no natural family connection.

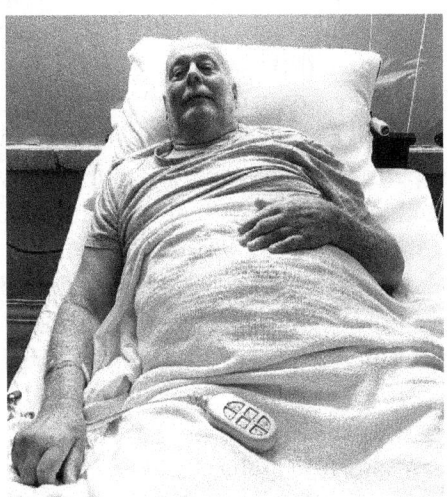

Wayne Scott in the Hospital

Bro. Vance Moore

Wayne is a gentle giant, a large man, quiet, and easy going. He grew up in Central Christian Church with his family: father, mother and sister. His dad was a deacon in Central. After his father passed in 2000, Wayne became a deacon.

When I arrived at Central in 2015, I was amused that Wayne is the greeter; he's so quiet and laid back! People are attracted to his quiet, gentle spirit. Wayne is as dependable as they come. In the five plus years I've been at Central I only remember one Sunday he missed being in the narthex passing out bulletins, and that was because his truck had broken down and he couldn't get to church. That's where my Wayne story starts—his second Sunday not being in church, June 30,2019. Everyone was surprised that Wayne wasn't there and during our time of announcements I asked the Board Chair to call and check on him. Calls were made and I later learned that several folks tried to call to no avail.

By Monday morning I knew that I needed to check on Wayne, so I headed to the country to check on him. The old home place is out of the way, 1500 feet off the road. Railroad construction in the late 1800's cut off access to the main highway and access is achieved by going north a quarter mile, crossing the tracks and coming back on a frontage road a quarter mile to the driveway. It's an interesting drive, especially if it's your first trip! Wayne is a lifelong bachelor, a man that loves to keep all the things that he's acquired over the years. Property maintenance is achieved by making the best of what he had to work with at the time. The old house is over 150 years old and in utter disrepair. That statement should help to paint the picture: Unique but definitely not Currier and Ives!

As I wound down the long gravel driveway, lined by trees that survived Hurricane Katrina, I wondered where in the world a house could possibly be. I truly was in the "boondocks." A short turn and all of a sudden I arrive at the house. His lawnmower has been broken, the grass is high and

Critical Presence: Love God, Love Y'all, That's All

junk all over the place. I see several barn cats hanging around the back door. Wayne's truck is parked close to the back door. I pull up, get out of my truck and walk to the back door. I can see through the screen door that the back door is slightly ajar. I felt chills as I realized that something was desperately wrong. I called his name, no response; I called his name again, this time loudly. I heard a faint sound coming from inside the house.

I called out, "I'm coming inside, it's Bro. Vance, where are you?" This time I heard no response. I went inside and found a cluttered house, dark, and it's hot (June in Mississippi it HOT). I go thru the washroom into the hallway, look into the bedroom, then in the dining room off the hallway. I saw chairs turned over.

As I stepped forward, I saw Wayne, on the floor, under the edge of the dining room table. Wayne was barely awake. Later the EMT's would tell me he was barely alive. In a barely audible voice and eyes barely open, Wayne said one word, WATER. I got him water and gave him a sip. It was obvious he was in severe medical distress. He wanted more and I gave him another sip and called 911.

They sent the volunteer fire department and EMT's with the ambulance. I had to go back to the frontage road and meet them. The mailbox is way over on the highway and the driveway is obscured by trees and grass, very difficult to see. EMT's arrived first and started what I now know and call "Wayne's miracle." It took two EMT's and five firemen to get Wayne off the floor, out of the house and into the ambulance for the fifteen mile ride to Forrest General Hospital.

In the emergency room we learn that at this time Wayne has no memory of what happened or how long he was on the floor with no food, no water, no air conditioning (he has no air conditioning in his home) and only one window fan in a room adjacent to the dining room. Later on, we learned that no one had seen him since the 26th, five DAYS before we found him.

Bro. Vance Moore

As his memory began to return he remembered going by the Rayburn's office the Wednesday before and then home. He remembers being extremely hot and thirsty. It was no surprise to learn that he was in renal failure. Wayne spent day one in the ER and then twelve days in the hospital. Wayne was a very sick man.

Then came dialysis and Wayne crashed. He told the Doctors he did not want dialysis, would not live like that and refused the procedure. At the same time, he refused to apply for Medicaid which would open up the possibility of payment for many of the services the Doctors believed he'd need in the time to come. It was a dark day.

After much conversation, prayer and common-sense prevailing, Wayne agreed to take a few dialysis treatments to see if his acute renal disease could be reversed. This meant moving him to a skilled nursing facility which would entail dialysis three times weekly. In addition to dialysis Wayne would need extensive physical and occupational therapy; he had not walked or even been out of the bed since I found him over two weeks ago.

The move was made to Bedford Center of Hattiesburg, a nursing home with rehab facilities. Wayne accepted care but showed little signs of believing he would recover. His depression was evident. His road to recovery was beginning in a dark place. Wayne truly was at his point of deepest need.

July 10 was day one in Bedford. Wayne has a sister living in Atlanta. She came over and spent a few days in the beginning, but had to return to Atlanta later on. Wayne decided to allow me to be his #1 Power of Attorney for his medical care and his sister to be the backup. This was done to allow us to help him make good decisions about next steps in his care and to create a day to day audit of health care with Bedford and the medical team.

I created "Team Wayne." Prayer Warriors from Central Christian, family (including the Rayburns), and anyone that

Critical Presence: Love God, Love Y'all, That's All

would listen to our cry for prayers. God sent me a helper. One of the elders from the church has helped me throughout the journey to recovery. We began visiting Wayne twice daily; I'm blessed, I live within a few blocks of Bedford. We would attend to little things that needed to be done, uplifting conversations, and prayer!

From the beginning, insurance and costs were looming. Wayne refused Medicaid and had very limited liquid assets. His fear was losing the small farm that had been in his family for generations. Medicare pays 100% first 20 days of care in a SNF and then 80% from days 21 to 100. After that it's Medicaid or private pay. Bottom line—Wayne needed to heal quickly or he'd lose what little he had saved in the 50+ years of working and eventually the farm would literally be in jeopardy. That coupled with the severity of his medical condition was a tremendous drain on his spirits.

We knew that only God could fix this. We knew that from day one! I knew that we were with Wayne at his point of deepest need and I knew that God had placed me there. This was a divine appointment, no doubt.

Each day was a challenge. Wayne is a big man; in the beginning he was around 300 lbs. and difficult for staff and physical therapy to handle. Yes, they're trained but 300 lbs is 300 lbs. Over a period of time his weight dropped to 243 and continues to decline. Diet, dialysis, and exercise are responsible for that blessing. As I write this, we are at day 82 and all treatments continue. Therapy is going well. Wayne is walking more and better each day. We are hopeful that dialysis can end soon and that Wayne can return home to rebuild his life!

The Rayburns have an apartment in town that they retrofitted to accommodate his needs during the next stage of his recovery. This story is a life event—a personification of "meeting people at their point of deepest need." Earlier, when we were serving at Westside after Hurricane Katrina, we coined a phrase, "It's a God Thang." Wayne's story is meeting people at their point of deepest need, serving the need (Critical Presence) and watching a "God Thang" happen.

I'll close this recanting of events with the thought I had the morning of July 1 when I found him near death on the floor of his dining room. I had no idea how it would play out, but I know that this was his "point of deepest need" and I knew that God had given me a "Critical Presence" divine appointment. It is my hope and prayer that you see the hand of God in this and that together we can give Him the glory for saving Wayne.

Wayne Scott

Critical Presence: Love God, Love Y'all, That's All

Wayne Scott's Old Home

We're getting ready to go to final print with Love God, Love Y'all, That's All. When I arrived at church this morning Wayne was there in the back as always. My first question was "How's the new house coming along?" Wayne has sold a few acres of the home place and the Rayburns are helping him build a small house to replace the dilapidated house he's lived in for so many years. I've included a picture. It's almost complete and it is a blessing!! Thank you Jesus.

Wayne Scott's New Home

Bro. Vance Moore

Now for the other FANTASTIC—WHERE DID I SEE GOD TODAY? I took a deep breath, said a silent please Jesus prayer and asked Wayne how his appointment with the dialysis clinic went this week? We've been waiting for months for the final answer on continuing dialysis! Wayne smiled and told me that the bottom line is all numbers have come in line and in tolerances. NO MORE DIALYSIS. I felt a tear as I walked away. I'm so blessed. God let me witness a miracle. He actually let me be a small part of the process. Not the ones we study in HIS word; one of HIS TODAY MIRACLES. Living proof that God is still in the miracle business. Thank You Jesus!! To God be the glory. He Lives, He Lives—Christ Jesus Lives Today.

Gloria M

I'd like to share another story about the fruits of the Spirit that conveys the very essence of Critical Presence. There is a former member of my church named Peggy. Peggy has a sister whose name is Gloria. Gloria was a psychiatric nurse who worked in Home Health Care. I met Gloria recently. As I write this today, she is now with our Lord Jesus in our forever home! The interesting part of this story is how I became involved in her life.

Peggy and her husband George became members of Central Christian Church in a little over a year ago. Even the way they came to us was interesting. I received a phone call one night and it was Peggy. She said, "I looked you up on the internet, through Facebook. I'm calling you because you pastor of a Disciples of Christ Church in Hattiesburg. I'm trying to locate a church that my husband George would be comfortable attending. We moved to Hattiesburg a couple years ago and we've been attending another church. It's not a Disciples church and it's a large church and he's not happy.

Critical Presence: Love God, Love Y'all, That's All

Because of that he's resisting attending and I know he needs to find a good church. Can you help me?"

I spoke with her for a few minutes that evening and basically said, "Come and see. If you like what you see stay. If not, move on in your search. The important thing is to find a church home where you can be a part of God's Church.

They came, they listened, they stayed and they joined.

Fast forward to the phone call from Peggy about Gloria.

"They are taking my sister to the hospital. She's had a heart attack. It's not good. I don't know what to do. I'm afraid."

We talked. I reached out to her with prayer and with an offer to help in any way I could. We made a decision to go visit Gloria as soon as possible. That possibility came about a week later after Gloria came home from the hospital.

Gloria lives in Bush, Louisiana, which is about an hour-and-a-half away from Central Christian Church in Hattiesburg, Mississippi. No matter the distance, my member needs us. So we go. Peggy, Gwen and I headed out on a Saturday morning to go down to visit Gloria. George decided not to go. We got to Bogalusa, Louisiana, which is about halfway between Hattiesburg and Bush. We got a phone call that says, "Mama is too sick for this visit."

We were hearing from David, her son, who was a paramedic before changing professions. He is now driving a school bus so that he can take care of his Mama.

We turned around and returned to Hattiesburg to do the only thing we know to do. We prayed.

Several days later we rescheduled the visit, only to have it interrupted again by Mama going to the hospital, having suffered another heart attack. I found out through a phone call from Peggy, who was on the way to be with her sister Gloria. I hopped into our car. I headed toward the hospital, not knowing what I would encounter when I got there.

My first face-to-face with meeting with Gloria was in the

Bro. Vance Moore

Saint Tammany Regional Hospital, Covington, Louisiana. She was very sick. The doctors had just shared with her family, that there was no hope. They were going to declare her to be a hospice patient. I had been there before. I knew exactly where we were. I walked into the room—the CCU. I saw a frail, fragile person, maybe 80 pounds. She looked like so many of the hospice patients I've seen.

I've left out part of the story, dating back to when Peggy first asked me to get involved. She told me she was unsure of whether or not her sister was saved. It troubled her greatly. Peggy and I sat outside the hospital on a bench as she revisited that need. That was why I was there. That's why I found myself standing at the bedside of another hospice patient. Boy, had I been there before. Even now, I don't know how to describe that experience. It is in moments like those that I feel the clear, undeniable closeness and the presence of Jesus Christ. The blessing of being able to be there at a person's time of deepest need is what we call Critical Presence. In many ways I'm reminded of Christ speaking to us in the Word and telling us, "Don't worry when you don't know what to say. My spirit will speak for you, will give you the words to say." It's times like those when I recognize the power of his words. I am humbled when I realized I've been allowed to be the one to share Critical Presence.

I met Gloria. I gazed at her face. I felt her pain. I sensed the Presence. She was easy on my heart. It was so easy, so comfortable to learn who this lady was.

When the time was right, I asked the question I came to ask, "Do you know Jesus?"

She says, "Yes!"

I looked directly into those beautiful blue eyes and I saw the nurse she had been throughout many years, serving Christ. I knew it was there. Still I knew I had to ask, that I had to be sure.

So I said to her, "Is it okay with you if I ask a couple of questions?"

Critical Presence: Love God, Love Y'all, That's All

She smiled at me and said, "Of course."

"I think I heard you say you did know Jesus Christ as your Savior. Is that true?"

She said, "Yes."

I asked, "He is your Lord?"

And she said, "Yes."

I saw the sparkle in her eye and I felt the connection. I knew we were a brother and sister in Christ. We had much to share. We began our acquaintance that day. I spent time with her, learned of her career of service and love—not only as a nurse, but as a loving Christian human being. I saw Critical Presence in action. We prayed. As I prepared to leave her side that day, I knew she and I would walk this path, this hospice path, together, as brother and sister in Christ.

It's really simple. I'm called to share stories like this. Critical Presence has been lived out by this beautiful lady I met in Saint Tammany Regional Hospital in Covington, Louisiana. In her quiet, sweet way, she shared with me a lifetime of service. A moment of deepest need drew me to hospice, and there I experienced Critical Presence, the time where "the rubber meets the road." Now, now, it's her turn. Deep Need, who's going to be there in her time of greatest need? Jesus has called me and said, "Here, my son, is a blessing for you. Be there for Gloria; living Critical Presence!"

Over the next few weeks and a couple of visits after they sent her home, our relationship deepened. The blessing bestowed on us as God provides a "Divine Appointment," that time when He places someone in your path to serve Him; it's really simple, I (you, we) surrender ourselves and allow Him to work through us to touch one of His children (or a sinner needing a relationship with Him). You/I become Him in service to carry the gospel, good news, message. All win, Love God happens in the only way it can; it originates with Him, permeates you in every way, teaching us to how to Love Him, Love Y'all (more about that later), That's All. Remember

Bro. Vance Moore

what Billy Graham said, "It's God's job to judge all situations and folk, OUR JOB TO LOVE. Oh, how sweet it is.

Well a little later on Gloria did go to be with the Lord; The family had me conduct the service. That little country church was full of lifelong friends and the love of Christ surely in the house of the Lord that day!

Peggy and George have since moved on; still looking for the church to which they feel called. Our prayer is that they find the peace of Christ. Makes me remember words I used in Gloria's service; words of Christ, *"I go now to prepare a place, so that where I am you may be also,"* Thanks You Father! Amen

Stuart and Howard E.

Following is a Facebook post from Stuart Irby, a Realtor, a Christian, a friend, a Brother in Christ.

There are days in my job that really get to me. Today was one of them.

I went to Prentiss today to a run-down house on a dirt road and had to tell this little old black man that his house was foreclosed on last week and I'd be the broker selling it for the bank.

We went over the paperwork on the hood of my truck. He then walked around the outside of the house with me and told me all about it and what all was wrong with it while I took pictures for my report.

We made it back around to my truck and he told me how he'd taken care of his mother in that house until she died and how he'd taken care of his father in his house until he died. He told me about how he'd gotten cancer and had to have a kidney removed and the medical bills and prescription costs had caused him to get behind on his house payments. He told

Critical Presence: Love God, Love Y'all, That's All

me about a vision he'd had during his fifty-seven days in the hospital. He was clear that he didn't actually see the face of God but that he'd seen his shadow.

Then this frail, little old man asked me how I was. He said he had seen me limping and could tell I was in pain. I told him I had just come from getting an MRI and that I was hoping this new doctor I am seeing is going to be able to help me.

We continued to talk for thirty minutes or more about how everything is God's plan and to keep a pure heart and we all have a purpose. As we said our goodbyes and I went to shake his hand, he took my hand in both of his, and with tears in his eyes, he prayed for ME.

The guy that just basically told him he was going to be kicked out of his home. Here's this frail black man, standing in the front yard of the home that he is going to end up being evicted from, tearfully praying for the white guy that was telling him he would have to be vacating soon. There was not one bit of animosity towards me. There was no racism, no politics, no division, no hate, no anger, no rage, no self-pity. There were only two children of God praying for one another in front of a run-down house on a dirt road in Prentiss, MS.

I really don't have the words to express how much this man touched me. I can't even tell you all the emotions that I'm feeling. I'm not sure I even know. He told me he never asks God, "Why?" His faith in God was so strong that even losing his home couldn't shake it. After all that he had lost and all the trials he had been through, his heart was still pure enough to pray for someone else. A complete stranger. Maybe there is hope for this world after all.

***

After I read this post, I contacted Stuart. I felt a strong, strong need to meet this man, to see his heart and to share his story.

Bro. Vance Moore

As soon as Stuart sent me some contact information, I called Howard E. I simply told him that I needed to come, meet him and pray with him. Howard did not hesitate, gave me his address and we set a time for me to come.

I had one member, Wayne S., in the rehab unit at Bedford Nursing home in Hattiesburg (twenty-five miles south Howard's home) and was on my way to visit Lisa R. in Jackson (eighty-five miles north of Howard's home). When I arrived I only had about one hour to visit and then had to leave.

We talked and Howard shared his story. I appreciated the dilemma he faced with the foreclosure of his property and shared with him that we had no money to help him. [Please note he has not asked anyone, to the best of my knowledge, for any money.] In fact he quickly shared with me that he had turned everything over to God, including the issues of foreclosure. His only regret was losing the family home and his hopes of living out his remaining days in the house that had been home for so long.

Our conversation quickly turned to faith and prayer. I looked into the eyes of a Brother in Christ; not a black man, in failing health, about to lose what little worldly things he has—NO—I stood eighteen inches from him holding hands and praying.

He had asked me to tell him about Wayne S. and Lisa R. and we prayed for each of them. I wept as we prayed—what unselfish strength I found in this man. I left with us having both found a relationship with each other thru Jesus Christ. Praise God. Just before I left he asked if I could let him pray with Wayne so he could share his love.

"You betcha," I said.

The next morning when we visited Wayne, I put Howard on speaker phone (lying on Wayne's chest) and he prayed for Wayne. It was a special blessing and a memory I'll cherish. That was several weeks ago.

I've been really busy and have heard from Howard. One

Critical Presence: Love God, Love Y'all, That's All

day last week my phone rang and it was Howard. He told me he'd had Wayne on his heart and asked after him. We shared good news and promised to stay in touch. Stuart posted on Facebook that some folks are trying to put some sort of help together to help Howard to be able to remain in the house.

I pray for him. Ain't God Great! I met Howard E at his point of deepest need—YES—and when I did, I found God standing with him in LOVE and STRENGTH.

As I write this, changes are happening. Stuart started a group that's working to buy Howard's house out of foreclosure; they will then, with the help of the local Habitat for Humanity, do the repairs that will make it possible to Howard to live in his earthly home until God brings him to his eternal home. Beauty is that my friend has worked hard to bring the love of Christ to Howard with the gift of his earthly home. Jesus has already prepared Howard's heavenly home. It's paid for!! Praise God. Amen

Bro. Vance Moore

Chapter Six
Critical Awareness Future

Meet Nae Nae

About two years ago one of our members restarted a dog therapy ministry. She had participated in this type of ministry several years ago and felt the call to restart. In dog therapy, people go to nursing homes with therapy dogs and visit the residents. She quickly had six to eight weekly participants working three Mondays each month in three to five nursing homes. I went to visit with them on occasion and thoroughly enjoyed the concept of dog therapy. It let me get in nursing home rooms and pray with patients.

Meet Glory

Critical Presence: Love God, Love Y'all, That's All

During that time I became a volunteer chaplain at Forrest General Hospital, a position I held for about six months until it became too much of a schedule conflict and I had to leave that ministry. Working in the hospital was very similar to our ministry at Yellow Pine. I loved being in the hospital environment in "deepest need" ministry. Ministry life was good and I was comfortable, but the "burning" to be involved with "deepest need" ministry was lacking.

In late September of 2018, we got an unusual request from one of our members: their granddaughter, a military veteran in her 30's was dealing with PTSD and had been taken to the Veterans Hospital in Biloxi, Mississippi. She left three dogs and a bird abandoned at her home in Sumrall, a small town about fifteen miles outside Hattiesburg.

The family needed some help with foster care for the animals, especially the bird. Our dog therapy lady knew someone in Columbia, Mississippi who worked with birds. With the help of a family member, the bird was retrieved. As the family member put the cage in the truck for transport, he tilted the cage and the bird escaped. They called me and we agreed to leave to cage in its home place with the door open and food inside, thinking it might return. I was dispatched the next morning just before daybreak to see if the ploy worked. It did not. Bird gone!

Along with my parishioner who did dog therapy, I found myself at the abandoned home of the veteran. This was my first trip and my first time to see the dogs. Though the family member had left some food for the three dogs, they had been in the yard with no food and only rainwater to drink for about two weeks since the veteran went to the hospital.

A little feisty breed came running to the gate, letting me know that I should be afraid of him since he might bite. Then there was the old collie—friendly, tired, filthy, but clearly a loving old dog. Arrangements had been made for someone to pick up those two, but there was one more—the main reason we were there.

Bro. Vance Moore

From around a large doghouse, dragging what could easily called a log chain, came a large, long-haired, white (dirty, nasty) dog with a look I'll never forget. Later I learned that she was already a rescue (our veteran had rescued her from someone else, though we never did find out where). The dog reminded me some of Buddy the cat, that I'd rescued in New Orleans. Deepest Need is deepest need, even dogs!

My friend and I pulled the chain stake out of the ground and loaded the dog into her SUV. That was on Saturday. On Monday I took the dog to the Vet to be checked out. By that time, we had cleaned her up and spent two days helping to begin her recuperation. Dr. Davis gave her a clean bill of health with the exception that she only weighed 68 lbs and her breed (Great Pyrenees) should weigh about 115 to 120 lbs. Within one week we learned that she would not be a temporary care "foster" but a permanent "rescue." We named her Naomi (biblical), that was shortened to "Nae Nae." All of a sudden I had a therapy dog. Literally within one week of rescue we took her to a nursing home with the other therapy dogs and she was a natural.

As I started going into long term care rooms, I began to remember a different side of health care. This was vastly different from Hospice care. Nae Nae helped me to carry Jesus to people who were starving for someone to love them, someone to just care. Their point of deepest need in many cases was having been forgotten. I don't want to leave out those in rehab units, people who have the possibility of going home, or those in long term care that have loved ones who visit regularly, or those still able to function at some reasonable level. I am talking about those bedridden, confined to wheelchairs, unable to function.

I'm talking about those that have exhausted all their resources and now are dependent on Medicaid—which simply means that any and all resources they have go to their housing and basic care. Even their social security checks goes to the

Critical Presence: Love God, Love Y'all, That's All

system which houses them. [Medicaid allows you to keep $44.00 per month for incidentals like a haircut or a beauty appointment.] We'll talk much, much more about these things as we go forward.

Nae Nae

I don't intend the focus of this book to be about the inadequacies of the health care system in the United States, but there has to be an awareness of end-of-life issues and the need to address this crisis. Rather, the focus of my message is the CRITICAL PRESENCE NEED TO TAKE THE LOVE

Bro. Vance Moore

OF JESUS CHRIST to those in whom Christ is speaking when He gives us His commandment to LOVE ONE ANOTHER.

I want to tell their story, thru my eyes and thru my heart and thru my passion. It is not enough to sit on the sidelines and talk about it. I must do something. It begins by letting them see Jesus thru a big old dog that knows firsthand what it means to be rescued because of love; it begins by having a brother (Bro. Vance, and then many more as we grow) sit at their bedside and share the love of Jesus in as many ways as God leads us.

It's so much **more** than just 'sitting at bedside'; it's building relationship, discovering needs (ways to help them and their families) in practical ways; and then duplicating my ministry by developing Timothies to go out into other facilities on a volunteer basis. I have no idea how big God wants this to be. I know the need is great and the workers may be few now, though I've got the feeling that God is going to bless me in my golden (remaining) years by letting me serve Him in a mighty way!

Chapter Seven
What is God's Will for You?

Matthew 5:45 tells us that God gives his sunlight to both the evil and the good, and He sends rain on the just and the unjust alike. In this verse, Jesus is saying life consists of both evil and good and that, as human beings, we will inevitably experience both.

I'm reminded of a book by Robert Schuller, *The Be-Attitudes* in which he deals with the question, "Why do bad things happen to good people?" In a very forthright manner, he states that the question instead should be, "What happens to good people when bad things happen?" Then in great detail he discusses what it means to have a relationship with Jesus Christ.

When we look at the citizens of New Orleans as it is, as with any other culture, we see there are good people and there are people who are not good. Hurricane Katrina was a precise example of exactly what Jesus declared in Matthew 5:45. The rain surely did fall on the just and the unjust. Natural disasters are a natural part of life. The overwhelming disaster that resulted from Hurricane Katrina occurred as a natural part of life. While it was not necessary for Katrina to occur in order for us to obey God's will for us, it did provide us the opportunity to show our love for our fellow man and our obedience to God.

As it's written in Matthew 22:37-40, "Jesus replied, "'You must love the LORD your God with all your heart, all your soul, and all your mind.' This is the first and greatest commandment. A second is equally important: 'Love your neighbor as yourself.' The entire law and all the demands of the prophets are based on these two commandments."

In our quest to understand the Bible as well as gaining a greater understanding of Jesus and our relationship to him, we often forget the simplicity of the Great Commandment. It is the will of God that we love our neighbor as we love ourselves. Serving by doing things that help to repair and relieve the pain and devastation of a natural disaster like Hurricane Katrina is a prime example of loving one's neighbor.

I find it interesting that the conversation about theist versus atheist many times can be handled and quickly elevated to a level that seems to be unresolvable. Logic and reasoning tell us that there is good and there is evil. To deny that there is good and evil implies a world situation so chaotic that the world as we know it simply could not exist. That may seem to be an overly simplistic view. Regardless, it is obviously, demonstrably true. Additionally it seems clear to me that we are all born with an innate sense of right and wrong. As such the idea of reaching out to others compassionately, I believe, is there inherently in all of us.

As I discussed earlier, I believe there are two concepts with which we are born with that drive us to believe in a Creator. One is creation itself, exemplified in the beauty of a sunrise, a sunset, and all the magnificence of things great and small. That is the physical proof of the Creator God, that aspect of the world that can be observed and measured by what we call science.

Second, man is also created with a conscience. While this reality is not part of what we deem natural science, it is nonetheless an integral part of the spiritual aspect of what it is to be a human being. Our revelation of and our relationship to Jesus Christ enhances our knowledge of the distinction between good and evil and our response to God's will. This is a clear element of the proof that man is born with a natural desire to discover the purpose, the meaning of our existence.

This is the "existence question." Down through the course

of human history, philosophers sought to answer the question, "What is truth?" Beginning in the middle of the 20th century, however, the basic question of philosophy became, "What does it mean to exist?"

For those who are spiritually open, those who hear and respond to the call of Christ, the answer to that question becomes obvious. God's Word states in the Book of Genesis, "Let us create man in our image." Because God is omniscient, omnipotent and omnipresent, we know God is all-sufficient, needing nothing. Therefore we know He created us because He chose too, not because He needed to. He created us in his image in order to serve Him.

In all of my studies and teachings, I asked my students, "What is the first memory you have of being asked, 'who is God'?" Without fail the immediate answer is always, "God is love." That leads to the discussion of how we were created out of love, to serve God in love by doing those things that reveal God's love. Whenever we reflect on that incredible truth, "No greater love can a man have than to give his life for his friend," one of Jesus' great lessons comes to mind. When we consider the profound depth of sacrificial love, it immediately reveals the point that everything that we read in the Bible centers around love.

Most of the volunteers who came to serve through the Westside Mission Center would tell you that I supervised very little, that I allowed them to do all they were asked to do without interference. I actually don't believe I allowed the volunteers to work without interference. I do believe that I allowed them the opportunity to do the very best they could given their talents and abilities. I believe as well that God worked with them and through them, empowering them to grow in their abilities as they served others.

Years ago I read a book written by A.L. Williams. At the time he was the CEO of Primerica Insurance Company. The name of his book is *All You Can Do Is All You Can Do, But*

Bro. Vance Moore

All You Can Do Is Enough. That's probably the longest title of a book that I've ever heard. Yet the entire little book carries forth that one thought.

Several significant points relating to our topic emerge from this powerful idea. First, the thousands of people who came in response to Hurricane Katrina were very diverse in age, education, vocation, ethnicity and even in their religious backgrounds. Some, not many, had construction experience. Most did not. What they did share was a longing to serve and a calling to reach out to help their fellow man. That longing was the God Thang!

Second, Hurricane Katrina brought devastation on a scale never seen before, not since and hopefully never again. Even those volunteers who had construction experience were faced with a type of work they had never encountered before. In addition to that they were going to work on property in New Orleans, an area unique in all of America. The houses they tore down and rebuilt, especially in the Lower 9th Ward, we're built during a time when there was little if any "industry standards."

A good example of this is the surprise expressed by many volunteers when they would came back from Home Depot with 2 X 4s to work on a house they were rebuilding, only to discover the actual measurement of the 2 X 4s they just bought at Home Depot were vastly different from the size of the 2 X 4s that were in the walls of the house they were working on. I can still hear Pastor Washington laughing. And then with his wry wit he would say, "They'll learn."

Third, certain aspects of the renovations had to be inspected by the city code inspectors. Those steps of renovation we came to had to do sometimes with licensed volunteers, but most often we required oversite by local licensed contractors. I'm speaking now of electric, plumbing and HVAC projects. We were able to do some very minor repairs, but always under the tutelage of locally licensed individuals.

Critical Presence: Love God, Love Y'all, That's All

Fourth, we have arrived at the God Thang side of this. As I reflect on my memories regarding this part of our work, it brings Don Miller to my mind. Don was from the St Louis, Missouri, area. He was a full-time contractor. He was also a youth minister. Don made around twenty separate trips to the Westside Mission Center. Each time he came, he would bring several people with him, people who were experienced construction folks. Often Don would work with the mission center's volunteers on my behalf.

Regarding this, I distinctly remember the "Mud Hens." This was a group of ladies who came and told me, "All we know how to do is cook, but we want to help. I had to share that with them that I had fifty volunteers and thirty cooks. Obviously we were going to have to find something else for them to do. At the same time, we were working on building the new sanctuary for Westside Christian Church. Don had come back to the mission center to hang and finish the sheetrock in the building. It needed to be done as professsionally as possible. Don was present when I had the conversation with the ladies.

I remember him laughing, looking at me and saying, "I'll teach them to finish sheetrock and we'll do it in the church."

I remember looking at him in disbelief. There were five of them—all five in total disbelief that they could do this. Still they wanted to serve and they said they'd give it their best. They worked and they worked and they worked. They applied the sheetrock mud and then sanded. And they sanded and they sanded until the sheetrock was smooth and professional in its appearance. Don was proud of them. I was proud of them. They were proud of themselves. They had gone beyond what they thought they could be, simply serving as cooks on a mission trip—something they already knew how to do. They had become, as Don named them, "Mud Hens."

That wasn't the end of their story either. The following year they showed up, each with a little kit of sheetrock finishing tools, and each possessing a hard hat with the inscription "Mud Hen," followed by her respective name. They came ready to serve, with willing hearts, open minds and profound faith. Critical Presence changes those who serve as well as those who are served.

In conclusion I guess it could be said—and it was said by some local officials—about all of the Westside volunteers, that we didn't always follow industry standards. The houses in the Lower 9th Ward were not built according to industry standards before the hurricane. Yet they stood the ravages of time until Katrina. Some of those houses had been there for over a hundred years, and they stand today: repaired, renovated and ready for the next hundred years. I challenge the thought that the volunteers did flawed work. Along with scores of homeowners ravaged by Hurricane Katrina, I am grateful and blessed with the work of the volunteers.

Yes, there were times that we had to redo some of the projects we had completed, but all of the work was done with love. I also would like to point out that on at least five occasions I was approached by homeowners who had been scammed and fleeced out of their money by contractors who did work so substandard that the homeowners, who had no money left, could not move back into their homes. Our Westside Mission Center volunteers whom I've written about removed the defective workmanship of the paid contractors and then—with love, patience and often their own money—rebuilt in love not only the damage caused by Katrina, but the corrupt projects done by unscrupulous contractors.

When it came to our volunteers, I know they all wanted to be part of the rebuilding effort, but I think very few expected the spiritual experiences that regularly embraced them. The "where did you see God today" time that we spent at the end of each day was extremely uplifting not only to me but to all the volunteers. My memory those meetings and the memories of the volunteers—ones I still hear from all these years later—

Critical Presence: Love God, Love Y'all, That's All

is of an experience of God's love in action that blessed the volunteers, the ones doing the work, much more than the blessings received by the recipients of their actions. Of course, when you talk to the recipients—the hurricane victims, their statement is that they received the most blessings.

By the way, this Pastor is sure that he also received the most lessons. I'm aware that much of the writing that I'm doing here has to do with Hurricane Katrina response. And that is as it should be. The efforts extended in Hurricane Katrina relief and rebuilding are a major part of *Critical Presence, It's a God Thang* and now with *Critical Presence: Love God, Love Y'all, That's All*. Yet as important and moving as the stories are about Hurricane Katrina, they're only part of the story.

In 2010 we closed the mission. I became full-time Regional Pastor, a position I held along with being the Director of Westside Mission Center since 2009. I traveled the entirety of the Great River Region for the next two years. I was asked as well to work with our mission effort to the Iglesia churches in the Dominican Republic. I went there and I experienced the same desire on the part of those congregations to reach out in faithful mission. In a part of the world where poverty and hardship are the order of the day, I saw amazing generosity and compassion in the name of Jesus Christ. Throughout my experience as Regional Pastor, as well as traveling throughout our nation and in the Dominican Republic, my experience taught me that those churches which were growing were the churches that were invested in volunteers and mission.

Regarding Central Christian Church in Hattiesburg, Mississippi, five years ago I was called serve Central Christian Church in. It was a small church, with fourteen dedicated, mature Christian members. Though they were struggling, they were dedicated. Conventional advice from the denomination—the larger church—was not optimistic for Central. It did

Bro. Vance Moore

not look as if they could continue for much longer. Each month, as they failed to meet the budget, they continued to deplete what resources they had.

Today, five years later, the church has twenty-five dedicated members—and mission is happening! Blessing bags are maintained, carried by several members of the church, and distributed to homeless people in the Hattiesburg area. The church supports Christian Services, an organization that deals with low income and the homeless in the Hattiesburg area. A group of ladies takes their therapy dogs to two nursing homes each month. Bible study is conducted weekly with a steady participation of eighteen individuals. Our Bible study is focused on how we can better carry the love of God to our brothers and sisters. We are actively, continually working for a deeper understanding of what it means to "be" Jesus, not simply to "hear" Jesus. The efforts of Central Christian Church are proof that volunteering through Critical Presence changes lives—the lives of those who receive our help, as well as the lives of those who volunteer. Volunteering is a central, essential part of serving Jesus Christ.

I wish the story could just go forward with only these parts in place. Sadly, there is more, MUCH more.

Chapter 8
Sanctuary

Where WE Experience Core Belief and Ordinances

Each Sunday morning I begin our worship service with a prayer. I don't use scripted prayer; never have. There is one part of the prayer that remains the same though: "Heavenly Father, we thank you for this beautiful Sunday morning. We thank you that we can walk through those front doors, and You are here. Lord we know that You are everywhere but this is special. We can walk through those doors and leave the outside outside! We can come into Your house and for just a little while we can be with You; feel Your love and grace. Thank You Father". Then I finish the prayer in various ways depending on what is going on in the congregation and what is on my heart. I often think about the meaning of that part of my prayer. It's at the heart of **Love God, Love Y'all, That's All.**

Praying about leaving the outside outside is NEVER an exclusive thing. You see, that's not who we are as God's people. I remember a time in my youth when the doors of the church were never locked. Anyone was welcome to come into God's house anytime they wanted too. Sadly, those days are gone. Back then the respect for His house pretty well assured no one would damage His house in any way. It is still reassuring that early every Sunday morning, we open the doors, put a sign out front that simply says welcome and we are ready to do just that; Members, visitors, seekers, anyone who wishes to come and worship with us is welcome.

Bro. Vance Moore

We practice **Love God, Love Y'all, That's All** period. We have our CORE BELIEF and yes we have our DOCTRINES; all grounded in respect, love, and a deep deep desire to follow His word in all we say and do.

Today Central Christian Church is an independent Christian Church. By that I mean that we are no longer affiliated with an organized denominational structure. We made that determination in 2019 based on our understanding/discernment of **Love God, Love Y'all, That's All**. Throughout our congregation there was an angst over the condition of the world in which we live and the lack of civil discourse. We see our Christian values being threatened in the public arena. It became obvious that we MUST stand up for what we believe. We needed to make our position known and crystal clear. We are a Bible believing church. Yes, there is much to learn, much to study, to discuss and yes, there are times we agree to disagree. I'll share more about that a little later on. First, I'd like to share our CORE VALUE with you. Our CORE value is the one thing on which we ALL BELIEVE, based on our faith. Our CORE value is simple to share and explain; Hear the words of Jesus:

"For God so loved the world that He gave His ONLY begotten Son, that whosoever believeth in Him should not perish, but have everlasting life." John 3:16 Simple, straight forward, written in language that all can understand. Yes, I know this is basic and simple. That's the point. The beginning point must be and is a simple understanding of the ONLY thing in which salvation of your soul and mine rests!

"For it is by GRACE you have been saved, through FAITH—and this is not from yourselves, it is the gift of God—not by works, so that no one can boast." Ephesians 2:8,9 Simply put but often misunderstood, works are a result of your becoming saved but they are not a part of how you are saved. Ephesians 2:8,9 is clear; there is one and only one requirement of salvation (*"whosoever believeth in Him"*) and that (*it is by*

Critical Presence: Love God, Love Y'all, That's All

GRACE you have been saved, through FAITH—and this is NOT FROM YOURSELVES, it is the gift of God, NOT BY WORKS).

There are other things, DOCTRINES, that we learn from God's word by reading, studying, meditation, prayer, sharing with each other in order to discern what His word is saying to us. It is important that we understand that these things are important:

"**Is salvation by faith alone, or by faith plus works?** This is perhaps the most important question in all of Christian theology. This question is the cause of the Reformation, the split between the Protestant churches and Catholic Church. This question is a key difference between biblical Christianity and most of the "Christian" cults. Is salvation by faith alone, or by faith plus works? Am I saved just by believing in Jesus, or do I have to believe in Jesus and do certain things?

The question of faith alone or faith plus works is made difficult by some hard-to-reconcile Bible passages. Compare Romans 3:28, 5:1 and Galatians 3:24 with James 2:24. Some see a difference between Paul (salvation is by faith alone) and James (salvation is by faith plus works). Paul dogmatically says that justification is by faith alone (Ephesians 2:8,9) while James appears to be saying that justification is by faith plus works. This apparent problem is answered by examining what exactly James is talking about. James is refuting the belief that a person can have faith without producing any good works (James 2:17,18). James is emphasizing the point that genuine faith in Christ will produce a changed life and good works (James 2:20-26). James is not saying that justification is by faith plus works, but rather that a person who is truly justified by faith will have good works in his/her life. If a person claims to be a believer, but has no good works in his/her life, then he/she likely does not have genuine faith in Christ (James 2:14,17,20,26).

Bro. Vance Moore

Paul says the same thing in his writings. The good fruit believers should have in their lives is listed in Galatians 5:22,23. Immediately after telling us that we are saved by faith, not works (Ephesians 2:8,9), Paul informs us that we were created to do good works (Ephesians 2:10). Paul expects just as much of a changed life as James does: "Therefore, if anyone is in Christ, he is a new creation; the old has gone, the new has come" (2 COR 5:17). James and Paul do not disagree in their teaching regarding salvation. They approach the same subject from different perspectives. Paul simply emphasized that justification is by faith alone while James put emphasis on the fact that genuine faith in Christ produces good works.

I hope this discussion has helped you to understand that we are not talking about doctrine here; rather we are discerning the very essence of our CORE belief. Without our CORE belief we are not Christians.

Now, on to the DOCTRINES. We don't always agree on the discernment aspect of scripture. We engage in civil, loving, respectful discourse to arrive at our personal application of the meaning of the truth in His word. There are even times when we embrace "agree to disagree", a statement which appeared at the death of George Whitefield. John Wesley wrote a memorial sermon which acknowledged but downplayed the two men's doctrinal differences. Rev. Wesley's quote, "There are many doctrines of a less essential nature ….In these we may think and let think; we may 'agree to disagree.' But meantime, let us hold fast the essentials." Later on Whitefield wrote, "After all, those who will live in peace must agree to disagree in many things with their fellow-laborers, and not let little things part or disunite them." I hope to be able to impart my deeply felt agreement with these words of 270+ years ago!

A little later on in the sanctuary service we come together and celebrate Holy Communion. As I prepare to offer the words of institution, I always say the same words of invitation,

Critical Presence: Love God, Love Y'all, That's All

"We come now to the time in our service where we come to the table of the Lord; the message of Christ is simple, 'ALL who wish to sup with Him are welcome.'". Simple words that convey succinctly the message that we have come to share. I'll expound on this in Chapter 9; suffice to say at this point that anyone who wishes to 'take' communion with us is welcome and invited.

Worship is the word that most churches use to describe the Sunday morning sanctuary service. I am somewhat amused at the different styles of worship governed both by denomination, by age of the worshipped, geographic area and economic dynamics. The dictionary says that worship is showing reverence especially in a spiritual sense and that is so true. How we as God's people live that out is exemplified by the 4000 different Christian denominations in the United States today. Makes me wonder how much of that worship style and practice is driven by 'doctrine'?

Bro. Vance Moore

Chapter 9
Big Tent

Ordinances of the Church

I heard a fellow once describe Christ church as a Big Tent under which we find the Lord's Table. His description pictured this Big Tent with each side rolled up and open so that anyone wishing to enter and approach the Table of the Lord could do so.

Recently I spoke about Troubled Waters, problems we face in life; all of us face in this earthly life. This past Wednesday, standing by a very cold graveside, the family wrapped in blankets provided by the funeral home, I spoke the words of Psalm 23. In doing so I said, "He leadeth me beside the still waters …He restoreth my soul." I said to the folks there at graveside, "Jean is not here, she's with Jesus"; I think now, she's passed over troubled waters, she passed by the still waters; she's in the arms of Jesus!

The story of that passage from troubled waters, then beside still waters to eternity with Christ is the story told under the Big Tent. It's the story of the Covenant of Love. It arrives in eternity, that place we call heaven, where we will live forever with God the Father, His Son Jesus, and the Holy Spirit! But before that we must go back before that place in Psalm 23 where He restores our soul, where we walk beside the still waters, and walk thru the "valley of the shadow of death"; that's the story of Troubled Waters; the story told under the Big Tent.

Before we step under the Big Tent this morning, let's spend a little time looking outside the Big Tent, in the world; there's two worlds actually, one natural and one super-natural;

Critical Presence: Love God, Love Y'all, That's All

we have to go thru this world (natural) to arrive at the Big Tent and be invited into the super-natural world (that's where Jesus is).

It's been mentioned many times, we live in a broken world.

We need now to step outside the doors of the church and look at the world we live in today. More than one group of well meaning Christians have used the mantra that we live in a broken world. I believe that and I think that you have only to turn on the 6 o'clock news any day of the week to agree with me. If we only take the time to look at the 'world' we live in we can see this as a new (old) problem.

I've had many of my members, friends and acquaintances tell stories of their younger days (back in the day). I'm almost happy I lived to the age that I can talk about 'back in the day'. Almost has a 'philosopher of sorts' sound to it, doesn't it? They're remembering days of our youth; simple days, days when our lives revolved around school, family and church. Yes Ma'am, No Ma'am, Thank You Ma'am, and Please were expected and given, no discussion. And I agree, but I think about another group of olden days. Back in the days of Adam and Eve, Cain and Abel, Esau and Jacob, Sodom and Gomorrah; now those were the olden days with civil discourse, disobedience, violent confrontation, hate. Days so filled with hate that it took a Savior to die on a cross and then be resurrected to pay the sin debt and defeat death.

As we read and study His word, it's easy to see the hate and evil that has been an integral part of mankind since the beginning of time after the Garden of Eden.

I guess it could be argued as to when we began 'our' slippery slope. Memories of the old days are probably better memories than reality, I know! Evil has existed since the beginning.

I am saddened by the realities of today. That sadness is not a memory. It's a reality.

Bro. Vance Moore

Today we have become a **polarized society**. We have reached a point in our interactions with each other that hate permeates our society. Civil discourse has become a thing of the past. No longer can we "agree to disagree". In almost every aspect of life there is only one way, one solution; and that way depends on what 'side' you're on. No longer do we have choices. The 'my way' or the 'highway' philosophy is the order of the day. And if you're not in agreement with me, you're the enemy. In order for one group to have their remedy, their rights, the opposing group has to give up their rights. No one wins in the end. No wonder we are living in a broken world. When one group has to lose for another to win, it never works. It is only when we strive to create a win-win that we'll begin to heal the broken world in which we live. Will we ever be able to live in a whole world? Maybe not, but, we can get a lot, lot closer; especially if we step under the Big Tent.

It's a monumental step we take, stepping under the Big Tent.

- Side of Searching—we step under the tent knowing there must be something better than the world outside, the natural world, the broken world, the world of hate. It's almost to say that if this is all there is I don't know if we can make it if something doesn't change.
- We see this Big Table under the Big Tent.
- We hear someone say, "This is the Lord's Table; all who wish to sup with Him are welcome . . .
- We come, we hear the message of a 'covenant of love'; where this Jesus' paid the price for all of our brokenness; where we can all win; no one has to lose.
- We decide this is where we want to be. We believe.
- Side of Others that have been here before

- We see many who have come before us. They heard about the 'covenant of love' but the brokenness of their lives pulled them back outside of the tent.
- Their pain keeps bringing them back. They are searching just like others; they're just not ready yet; but they keep coming.
- Side of the Fallen
  - We see many others that came and heard the 'covenant of love'. They believed. They spent many blessed days at the table 'supping' with the Lord, enjoying the 'covenant of love'.
  - Something happened and they took their eyes off the Lord. They stopped coming to the table; stopped receiving the 'peace that passes' all understanding they received at the Table of the Lord.
  - Soon they ended back outside the tent, back living in brokenness, back where losing is a way of life.
  - Now they come thru their side and approach the Lord's Table and accept those precious words, "All who wish to sup with the Lord are welcome"
- Side of the Faithful
  - These are those who came, those who heard, those who believed, those who accepted the invitation.
  - These are the believers, the saved, the servants.
  - They are the ones that once were broken, but have been made whole.

What is the message?

Bro. Vance Moore

- ➢ The natural world is a world without Christ, a world of brokenness, of hate, of division, of polarization.
  - o The natural world has existed since the time Adam and Eve achieved brokenness by **choosing** to disobey God. Mankind has lived in brokenness since.
  - o The brokenness, hate, division, polarization predominant in the world today is a **CHOICE**.
- ➢ The super-natural world is under the Big Tent. Christ says:
  - o *[16] "For God so loved the world, that he gave his only begotten Son, that whosoever believeth in him should not perish, but have everlasting life."* [John 3:16] (KJV)
  - o *"Come to me, all you who are weary and burdened, and I will give you rest. [29] Take my yoke upon you and learn from me, for I am gentle and humble in heart, and you will find rest for your souls. [30] For my yoke is easy and my burden is light."* [Matthew 11: 28]

Communion is not just a time for self-examination but Jesus-examination. The only thing that will empower you to overcome the natural world of brokenness is the grace of God. Look to Jesus. His blood bought your forgiveness and his resurrection from death on the cross triumphs over all your sin.

Critical Presence: Love God, Love Y'all, That's All

The next time someone says "communion is only for the worthy," don't be distracted by your sin; see Jesus who died for you.

Look at the Big Tent—: Thru which side do you enter?
- ❖ Seeking a way out of brokenness—hear the invitation to sup with Christ, hear His story, accept His salvation by faith through the grace of God
- ❖ Fallen—stand up—'fess up—WELCOME HOME
- ❖ Faithful—Love God, Love Y'all, That's All

"Yes, communion is for the worthy, and Jesus makes me worthy."

Christ at His Table still has more to teach His Church about who we are and what we are to do. Through sharing in the Lord's Supper, Christ shall continue to shape and reshape His church. Within the covenant of love we shall one day find ourselves fully at one with Him and one another.

Communion is when we remember Jesus' death on the cross. So who's it for? Obviously, it's for all those he died for, meaning everyone.

In the old covenant, sinners and unclean people were kept far away lest they contaminate the righteous. If there had been communion back then, they would not have gotten it! But Jesus was a friend of sinners. He went into their houses and broke bread with them. He met with thieves, adulterers and murderers and "contaminated" them with his righteousness. Sinners were radically changed by his awesome grace.

By saying "communion is only for the worthy" we have turned a new covenant blessing into an old covenant curse and denied grace to those who need it most. If communion is only for the deserving, who can qualify?

Jesus is still a friend of sinners! He died for us while we were sinners and he reconciled us to God while we were his enemies (Rom 5:8,10). People who hesitate over communion – both saints and sinners – do so because they are distracted by their imperfections. They draw back like Old Testament lepers because they believe that they are unclean. But you have been redeemed by the precious blood of Jesus (1 Pet 1:19). If God loves you enough to die for you, then in his eyes you must be really something special. And you are!

Ordinances of the Church

Make no mistake—there has always been only one requirement for salvation and we stand on firm foundation—belief in Jesus Christ—saved by Grace thru Faith.

We have touched on the journey that brought us to The Big Tent and under that Big Tent we meet and accept Jesus Christ as our risen Savior. There's journey forward and the Ordinances of the Church point the way.

Now, let's look at baptism and communion. What are they and how do they impact our lives as the "blood bought children of God" that we became the moment we believed? To begin this part of the journey, we must ask a question.

"Are baptism and communion means of grace?"

Answer: Quite simply, baptism and communion are separate from grace and are not a means to it. The rituals of the church do not confer grace, and they cannot merit salvation. It would be more proper to say the ordinances are he *signs* of grace, not the *means* of grace.

Water Baptism is not a means of grace; it is the outward expression of an inner change. It is an act of obedience *after* salvation has occurred. The examples of water baptism in Scripture all show that baptism happened after the person was born again (e.g., Acts 8:26-39). Being immersed in water (or

Critical Presence: Love God, Love Y'all, That's All

being sprinkled with water) cannot change a person's *heart*; that is the Spirit's work. "The Spirit gives life"(2 COR 3:6). Crucial to our salvation is faith in the heart, not water on the skin.

Communion or the Lord's Supper is not a means of grace; it is a memorial of Christ's once-for-all sacrifice and a picture of our fellowship with Him. At the Last Supper, when our Lord shared the Passover with the disciples, He said, *"This is my body given for you; do this in remembrance of me"* (Luke 22:19). Jesus was telling them (and us) not to forget His sacrifice on the cross. It was Christ's death that provided the remission of mankind's sin. There is never a word in Scripture about forgiveness or saving grace being applied through taking communion.

Paul also bears out the fact that communion is a memorial and not a means of grace: "Whenever you eat this bread and drink this cup, you proclaim the Lord's death until he comes" (1 COR 11:26). Eating the bread and drinking the cup are acts of obedience to the Lord, but they not a means of grace.

Grace, by definition, is free. It cannot be earned (Romans 6:23). The danger in saying that God's grace comes to us through a "means" or a "channel" of human activity is that it subtly mixes works with grace, something Paul warned against in Romans 11:6 The teaching that grace comes through baptism or communion is a sacramental view of the ordinances, and it undermines the meaning of grace. Grace is a free gift bestowed on the underserving. Sacramentalism says, "Unless you do these things, you don't get the grace." And that's tantamount to saying you must earn salvation.

The Roman Catholic Church claims to teach salvation by grace; however, Catholicism tempers that doctrine by also teaching that God's grace channeled through the sacraments. In other words, baptism and the Eucharist are two of the means of grace—through those rituals God gives the grace to eventually save a person. Receiving the sacraments will merit God's grace; no sacraments, no grace.

To teach that we are saved by grace is biblical. But to then qualify that teaching by requiring a ceremonial "means of grace" is double-talk. The biblical definition of *grace* specifically excludes human effort: "If by grace, then it cannot be based on works; if it were, grace would no longer be grace" (Romans 11:6). If grace only comes via religious deeds we perform, then it cannot truly be called "grace." <u>Any time we add human effort to Christ's work on the cross, we imply that Jesus' death was somehow, in some degree, insufficient to save.</u>

Thus, grace and works are mutually exclusive. Baptism is a work. Receiving communion is a work. We are not saved by works (Ephesians 2:8). Those who have been saved by grace will obey the Lord—saved people will be baptized, and saved people will take communion. In this way, the ordinances are "signs of grace"—evidences of a new life. They are not means of grace.

Religion always seeks a work to do. But Jesus is our rest (Matthew 11:28; Hebrews 4:10). His finished work on the cross and the regeneration of the Holy Spirit in the heart are what saves. Some men came to Jesus once and asked, "What must we do to do the works God requires?" (John 6:28). Jesus did *not* tell them to be baptized or to take communion. Rather, Jesus pointed to faith as the only "means of grace": "The work of God is this: to believe in the one he has sent" (John 6:29).

Chapter Ten
It's a Journey

Today Christians are confronted with a problem in regard to the Bible we have yet to solve. It is clear from our heritage that we have been taught to use our powers of discernment to interpret the scriptures. At the same time, we believe the Bible should be accessible and understandable to all people, not just scholars.

Biblical study has morphed into an exercise that excludes many of us "common folk." If we're not careful, Bible study has become an exercise that leaves us longing for simplicity, meaning and direction. We long to be confronted with the Living Jesus, our Messiah.

Today, you can still pick up the Book, the B.I.B.L.E. (Basic Instruction Before Leaving Earth), read it and find the Living Christ. The need today is the same it has been—approach the Bible with what Alexander Campbell called, "understanding distance." That is, with the humility of a child. It is when we approach the Bible with the desire to know Christ and serve Him that we find Him.

I love the Bible. It wasn't always that way. Make sure you hear that I've always respected the Bible. My upbringing and experiences have always been in knowing that the Word of God was, is and forever will be TRUTH, 100% TRUTH. Don't misunderstand me, I don't judge you if you don't feel that way. I just want to share with you my beginning point. Believing the Bible to be 100% true presented me with a conundrum that lasted for years. Still causes me to stop in wonder: how can I be so wrong when I first read a scripture? How can I now understand those words with the humility of a child?

Bro. Vance Moore

It helped several years ago when a good friend asked me how to study the Word. Answering his question sent me on a search to learn how to study the Word. Yes, investigative questions help: Who, What, When, Where, Why and How; then Context. All aids that flooded me with information—and I dare say knowledge, but something that quickly became a "go to" today. It's really simple, "Does what I'm discerning fit who I know God to be?"

Later on, I was studying and found myself looking at Matthew 22:34-40—*"Hearing that Jesus had silenced the Sadducees, the Pharisees got together. One of them, an expert in the law, tested Him with this question: Teacher, which is the greatest commandment in the Law? Jesus replied: Love the Lord your God with all your heart and with all your soul and with all your mind. This is the first and greatest commandment. And the second is like it. Love your neighbor as yourself. All the Law and the Prophets hang on these two commandments."* That bolstered my "God filter" by which I discerned the meanings in scripture. If it did not fit my 'God filter' I knew I needed to drill down in my study until I found the real God, the God of love.

My God filter shaped how I view life. Seems that my worldview is in direct relation to my God filter. I want to close this book by sharing my journey from God filter to worldview.

What is it, this thing we call worldview? Siri says it is "a particular philosophy of life or conception of the world." Hurricane Katrina gave me my first epiphany moments about worldview. I had been involved in ministry and mission for several years and yet my eyes were opened in New Orleans. I witnessed and lived out what I'll call "Mission without Walls." I saw people come together—virtually no prejudice, no racial barriers, no economic barriers; just a hurting world, needing help! For almost five years I was blessed to manage Westside Mission Center. In my first book, Critical Presence, It's a God Thang, I tell the stories of the people of New

Critical Presence: Love God, Love Y'all, That's All

Orleans and their struggle to overcome one of the greatest disasters our country has ever experienced and I share the experience, strength and hope of thousands of volunteers from all across the United States (we even had some exchange students from China) as they came week after week to help rebuild. Simply put, the people of New Orleans were suddenly faced with their "point of deepest need" and the volunteers responded to that "point of deepest need" as Christian Brothers and Sisters. I was forever impacted with the unbiased, non-prejudicial Love, GODS LOVE, agape love. No hate, no division, only sleeves rolled up, let's go to work and bring the love of God to our fellow man. Talk about Love God, Love Y'all, That's All. Here 'tis!

Worldview—What happened? What changed? In a few short years we've gone from discovering point of deepest need and striving to serve that need to an inability to come together in a civilized manner to even approach the need. I want to be crystal clear here. I'm not trying to diminish social justice/injustice issues in any way. Issues of bias, prejudice and injustice have been with us for as long as the human race has existed. What pains me deeply is the polarization of society and the hate that permeates the public arena. No longer can we have an opinion different from others; no longer can we disagree, without major hate, divisiveness and even violence. We can't agree to disagree. Civil discourse has become a concept not understood or practiced in the public arena. How sad. What happened? How did we become divided? It's not the issues—they remain the same; they need to be resolved. Progress has been and is being made on all fronts. Much remains to be done. That's not the issue. It's how. Why can't we approach each other and our differences with our thoughts and actions couched in love versus hate? I attended meetings within my ministry circle. Meetings that forced me to look at the worldview of those with whom I had been aligned for many years. It was then that I began to realize

Bro. Vance Moore

that the problem with many worldviews.

Worldview: I did what works for me. I went to the foot of the cross. I asked my Savior for Wisdom. I felt His Love. It became crystal clear. What is being done to solve the problems of social injustice or any injustice can only be accomplished in listening to His Words, *"Love the Lord your God with all your heart and with all your soul and with all your mind."* Then *"Love your neighbor as yourself."* As I struggled with my worldview, I realized that Jesus had already given the complete answer to this conundrum: we, as God's people can only heal the problems of injustice when we obey this command. I'd known that for a long time. It was only when I looked back to a time when it worked that I saw. During the time I served Westside Mission Center with people at their point of deepest need by people wanting to *"Love your neighbor as yourself"* by serving their neighbor; that was when it worked.

As I pen these words I hear in my heart—*"I look to a day when people will not be judged by the color of their skin but by the content of their character."* We all remember this MLK quote. It reminded me also of a sign in front of a church, "Jesus did not come to save skin color. He came to save souls." Each day, as we went about doing the work of serving people at their point of deepest need, I saw Him, I saw Jesus and if you're looking at Jesus, you don't see prejudice and hate. You see love.

Where do I stand—Love God, Love Y'all, That's All. How do I (we) live that simple but powerful "Great Command?"

Pray: Be honest with yourself about believing. Study Mark 9:23-25 *"'If you can'?"* said Jesus. *"Everything is possible for one who believes."*

Critical Presence: Love God, Love Y'all, That's All

²⁴Immediately the boy's father exclaimed, "I do believe; help me overcome my unbelief!"²⁵ When Jesus saw that a crowd was running to the scene, he rebuked the impure spirit. "You deaf and mute spirit," he said, "I command you, come out of him and never enter him again."—is there a lesson there for you? The Bible has all the answers. Read, study, pray—ask for understanding.

Understand: Do the things you think and do "fit" into your God filter. If it's not within you understanding of God, why is it in your life?

Action: Matthew 7:12 *"So in everything, do to others what you would have them do to you, for this sums up the Law and the Prophets."* If you are penalizing or disparaging any person or group in favor of another for any reason, go back and look Matthew 7:12 and 22:34-40.

Submit: Matthew 11:*29 "Take my yoke upon you and learn from me, for I am gentle and humble in heart, and you will find rest for your souls."* Are you doing anything that is polarizing, divisive, hateful, spiteful, prejudicial towards any of your fellow man? Have you submitted to His yoke?

I've given you just enough scripture to give you my worldview. I hope this will be the beginning of your journey to worldview. I am convinced and convicted that we must resist evil in all its forms. Our only hope lies in Jesus and His love.

www.ingramcontent.com/pod-product-compliance
Lightning Source LLC
Chambersburg PA
CBHW070622050426
42450CB00011B/3105